RAND NATIONAL DEFENSE RESEARCH INSTITUTE

T0290567

The Relationship Between Disability Evaluation and Accession Medical Standards

Heather Krull, Philip Armour, Kathryn Edwards, Kristin Van Abel, Linda Cottrell, Gulrez Shah Azhar

Prepared for the Office of the Under Secretary of Defense for Personnel and Readiness

For more information on this publication, visit www.rand.org/t/RR2429

Library of Congress Cataloging-in-Publication Data is available for this publication.
ISBN: 978-1-9774-0229-5

Published by the RAND Corporation, Santa Monica, Calif.
© Copyright 2019 RAND Corporation
RAND® is a registered trademark.

Support RAND
Make a tax-deductible charitable contribution at
www.rand.org/giving/contribute

www.rand.org

Preface

Anyone who is interested in enlisting in a military service undergoes a series of evaluations, including a medical examination. A military entrance processing station (MEPS), which is where the medical examination and other assessments take place, evaluates the recruit's health and fitness against U.S. Department of Defense (DoD) and military service accession standards. These standards change over time, which means that the timing of a recruit's visit to the MEPS determines how strict the medical requirements are that he or she must meet. Recruits who are evaluated under a tighter standard and who are permitted to join are healthier, on average, at the time of enlistment than those who join under less restrictive standards. The strictness of the medical standard at the time of evaluation, and the overall corresponding health of recruits who enlist under the policy, can be correlated with future health and career outcomes.

One potential career outcome is being medically discharged from military service with a disability. Service members who become injured or ill while serving can be referred for evaluation in the disability evaluation system. Prior to 2007, DoD and the U.S. Department of Veterans Affairs separately evaluated a service member's disability, but, in 2007, the two departments began implementing a joint program called the Integrated Disability Evaluation System. The system was fully adopted across DoD by the start of fiscal year 2012. Two adjudicating boards determine whether the service member meets medical retention standards and whether he or she is fit to continue serving. If neither of those outcomes is true, the service member is either medically separated (for an overall DoD disability rating of less than 30 percent) or medically retired (overall DoD disability rating of 30 percent or more). The costs to DoD of a medical discharge are numerous, including the loss of the service member's talent and accumulated skills, the need to replace that service member or retain another, and the cash compensation and medical benefits that are paid—for a lifetime, in the case of medical retirement.

During this study, we first examined whether a relationship exists between changes in accession medical standards and disability outcomes. Then, we developed a model to estimate the costs to DoD associated with these changes in accession medical standards. The results of this analysis will be of interest to DoD and service disability evaluation policymakers, including the Accession Medical Standards Working Group, for its reviews and revisions of accession medical standards and the Retention Medical Standards Working Group that is developing DoD-wide retention medical standards, and the DoD Disability Advisory Council. In addition, the findings will be useful for military medical and personnel communities, those who track and set targets for medical readiness, service waiver authorities, U.S. Military Entrance Processing Command and MEPS staff who implement accession medical standards, officials who plan and budget for disability evaluation, and the Department of Veterans Affairs for its role in maintaining the Integrated Disability Evaluation System.

This research was sponsored by the Office of the Under Secretary of Defense for Personnel and Readiness Office of Warrior Care Policy and conducted within the Forces and Resources Policy Center of the RAND National Defense Research Institute, a federally funded research and development center sponsored by the Office of the Secretary of Defense, the Joint Staff, the Unified Combatant Commands, the Navy, the Marine Corps, the defense agencies, and the defense Intelligence Community.

For more information on the RAND Forces and Resources Policy Center, see www.rand.org/nsrd/ndri/centers/frp or contact the director (contact information is provided on the webpage).

Contents

Figures

Tables

Summary

After speaking to a recruiter and completing initial screening, someone interested in enlisting in the military visits a military entrance processing station (MEPS) for further evaluation, including an aptitude test and a medical examination. The medical examination consists of a pregnancy test; blood-pressure screening; assessments of pulse, audio health, visual health, orthopedic health, and neurological health; a routine physical exam; and testing for human immunodeficiency virus, drugs, and alcohol. Those who pass the exam and meet all other requirements are permitted to join the military. Anyone who fails one or more components of the medical evaluation may enlist only upon receipt of a waiver for any identified condition.

The standards that are used during the medical examination are set by the U.S. Department of Defense (DoD) and the military services. These accession medical standards change over time, and the policy in place at the time of the medical exam dictates the requirements the recruit must meet. Someone who enlists under stricter standards will be healthier, on average, at the time of accession, than someone whose medical exam occurred during a period of looser standards.

One way to evaluate whether accession medical standards reflect the likelihood that service members will be able to withstand the rigors of military service is by following them over their careers to observe whether they incur injuries related to the medical standards that were in place at the time of their medical examinations at the MEPS. In particular, someone who suffers an injury or illness that impairs the ability to serve can be referred by the treating provider for disability evaluation.[1] Today, DoD and the Department of Veterans Affairs jointly run the IDES, which determines whether the service member meets medical retention standards and whether the member is fit to continue serving. If not, the service member is awarded a disability rating for the disabling condition(s) and discharged from the military.

In this study, we examined whether service members whose medical exams occurred after a change in accession medical standards had different rates of medical

---

[1] Throughout this report, we use the word *disabled* or *disability* in reference to a condition identified and rated through the DoD disability evaluation system or the DoD–U.S. Department of Veterans Affairs Integrated Disability Evaluation System (IDES).

discharge from those whose exams happened before the policy change.[2] We examined cases in which the policy change involved more-restrictive standards and cases in which the standards were relaxed. If the standard for a particular medical condition was tightened, for example, someone subject to the new standard might be less likely to have an injury associated with that condition and therefore less likely to be medically discharged with a disability rating for it. We then estimated how these changes in the number of service members who are medically discharged affect (either increase or decrease) the postservice costs to DoD.

The first step in this analysis was to identify when medical standards changed.

Accession Medical Standard Policy Review

The MEPS evaluates a potential recruit's medical status against DoD Instruction (DoDI) 6130.03, *Medical Standards for Appointment, Enlistment, or Induction in the Military Services*, which standardizes physical and medical requirements and provides definitions for medical conditions (Office of the Under Secretary of Defense for Personnel and Readiness [OUSD(P&R)], 2011). We reviewed changes to this instruction between 2000 and 2012 to align with our data analysis. During this study period, this instruction was issued or updated five times: in 2000, 2004, 2005, 2010, and 2011 (Office of the Assistant Secretary of Defense for Health Affairs, 2000, 2004a; OUSD[P&R], 2005b, 2010c, 2011). We compared the five versions of the DoDI and identified ten policy changes to include in our analysis. Of these ten cases, three standards were relaxed from their previous iterations, and seven were tightened.

The Relationship Between Changes to Accession Medical Standards and Medical Discharges

Our assessment was based on individual service member data from the Defense Manpower Data Center and the services, for all active-component enlisted service members who were accessioned between fiscal years 2002 and 2011.[3] Since 2012, 79 percent of all cases referred for disability evaluation have been active-component enlisted service members, so we selected this group as the focus of our analysis. For each year of service (YOS) for each member, we recorded individual demographic characteristics, service characteristics and experiences, and some basic information about where the member's medical examination was conducted. We also documented whether members were

---

[2] A *medical discharge* can be a medical separation (disability rating of less than 30 percent) or medical retirement (disability rating of at least 30 percent). Collectively, they are medical discharges.

[3] *Enlistment* means that someone has signed a contract, although that enlistee might not ship for training. *Accession* means that the enlistee shipped for training and actually shows up as part of the military's strength.

medically discharged, in what year, and when they left active-component enlisted service through any other channel, such as voluntary separation. We used these data to evaluate whether the policy changes we identified were correlated with changes in disability outcomes.

Our baseline analysis measured medical retirements (an overall DoD disability rating of 30 percent or more) in the first five YOS. Medical retirements represent two-thirds of all medical discharges. For each of the changes to accession medical standards that we evaluated in this study, we looked at service members who were medically retired for disabilities that mapped to medical conditions for which accession medical policies had either tightened or loosened. We included in our analysis service members whose medical evaluation occurred right before and right after the policy change, and we followed them to see whether those whose exams happened right after the policy change had different disability outcomes from those whose exams happened before. In doing so, we were able to determine the relationship between policy changes and medical retirements.

Figure S.1 shows the baseline results for medical retirements occurring during the first five YOS, which represent approximately half of all disability retirements that occur in a career. The numbers represent the percentage-point decrease or increase in five-year medical discharges for the prepolicy and postpolicy groups. Our analysis shows that accession medical standards are correlated with the probability of medical retirement, even after controlling for a rich set of individual characteristics and service experience. This effect varies substantially across services.

We examined three standards that loosened requirements: asthma, skin and cellular, and orthotics. Our results suggest that loosening these standards did not increase subsequent medical retirements due to a condition related to the standard change. Standards that were tightened, however, led to a statistically significant reduction in downstream medical discharges.

Abdominal medical standard changes consistently had significant effects, with the 2004 tightening of these standards reducing medical discharges in the Marine Corps by 0.09 percentage points and by 0.03 percentage points in the Navy. The 2005 abdominal standard change was correlated with a reduction of 0.03 percentage points across the Marine Corps, Navy, and Air Force. However, this standard change did not have a significant effect in the Army. The 2005 endocrine tightening led to a small but statistically and policy-significant reduction in related medical retirements for the Marine Corps.

The tightening of the skin and cellular medical standards in 2005, which required any applicant with psoriasis to receive a waiver, also led to a statistically significant reduction in the probability of being medically retired with a related disability. This restriction had the largest effect in the Army, reducing the number of skin-related medical retirements by 0.15 percentage points, with smaller reductions of 0.06 percentage points in the Marine Corps and 0.03 percentage points in the Navy.

Figure S.1
**The Relationship Between Changes in Accession Medical Standards and the Five-Year
Medical Discharge Rate for Those with at Least 30-Percent Ratings**

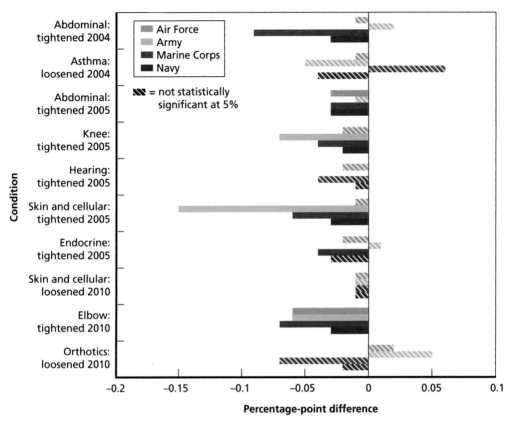

SOURCE: An analytic file made up of DMDC data, Veterans Tracking Application, and service disability
data.
NOTE: The year for each condition indicates the year the governing instruction was published. The bars
represent the percentage-point difference in the number of five-year disability retirements for service
members who were accessioned after the policy change and those who were accessioned before the
change. The five-year disability retirement rate is the percentage of service members who were medically retired by the end of the fifth YOS. To interpret these results, consider a group of 10,000 active-
component enlisted service members who were accessioned after the policy change. The effect of the
policy change is the effect shown, multiplied by 10,000. For example, the five-year estimate of knee-
related disability retirements for the Army is –0.0713 percentage points, which means that the marginal
impact in non–percentage point terms is –0.000713, so the estimate implies that there are 0.000713 ×
10,000 = 7 (rounded down from 7.13) fewer active-component enlisted soldiers who were medically
retired with knee-related discharges after the knee standard was tightened in 2005.

Finally, the 2010 tightening in the elbow range-of-motion standard was associated
with a reduction in the number of related medical retirements of at least 0.06 percentage points across all services except the Navy, which experienced a 0.03-percentage-
point reduction.

To convert these estimates into the number of service members affected, all effects reported in Table S.1 can be multiplied by the size of the accession cohorts in the years following the policy change. To standardize this interpretation, we multiplied each of the results in Figure S.1 by 10,000, which represents the following: For every 10,000 active-component enlisted service members who were accessioned after the policy change, that many more or fewer would be medically retired with a Veterans Affairs Schedule for Rating Disabilities corresponding to the policy. Table S.1 summarizes these results for a hypothetical group of 10,000 service members who were accessioned after each of the policy changes examined. To put these results into context, Table S.1 also includes the size of each service's active-component enlisted

Table S.1
The Relationship Between Changes in Accession Medical Standards and the Number of Five-Year Medical Discharges with at Least 30-Percent Ratings, per 10,000 Service Members

Group	Army	Marine Corps	Navy	Air Force
2004				
Active-component enlisted accessions	72,710	30,156	39,416	33,690
Abdominal (tightened)	2	−9**	−3**	−1
Asthma (loosened)	−5	6	−4	−1
2005				
Active-component enlisted accessions	63,324	32,015	37,729	19,092
Knee (tightened)	−7***	−4***	−2**	−2
Abdominal (tightened)	−1	−3***	−3***	−3***
Hearing (tightened)	0	−4	−1	−2
Skin and cellular (tightened)	−15***	−6***	−3***	−1
Endocrine (tightened)	1	−4***	−3	−2
2010				
Active-component enlisted accessions	70,081	28,018	34,048	28,363
Elbow (tightened)	−6**	−7**	−3***	−6**
Skin and cellular (loosened)	−1	−1	−1	−1
Orthotics (loosened)	5	−7	−2	2

SOURCES: OUSD(P&R), 2004, Table B-1; OUSD(P&R), 2005a, Table B-1; OUSD(P&R), 2010a, Table B-1.
NOTE: For every 10,000 service members who were accessioned after a policy change, we show the number we estimate will be medically discharged within five years with a disability related to the policy change more or fewer than those who were accessioned before the policy change. The five-year disability retirement rate is the percentage of service members who were medically retired by the end of the fifth YOS. ** = statistically significant at 5%; *** = statistically significant at 1%.

Table S.2
Cost Estimates and Percentage Changes in Cost from the Baseline That Are Associated with Accession Medical Standard Changes in the First Five Years of Service, per 10,000 Service Members

Condition	Change	Army		Marine Corps		Navy		Air Force	
		Amount, in Dollars	Percentage	Amount, in Dollars	Percentage	Amount, in Dollars	Percentage	Amount, in Dollars	Percentage
2004									
Abdominal	Tightened			−4,809,000	−0.55	−1,495,000	−0.17		
2005									
Knee	Tightened	−4,333,000	−0.49	−2,124,000	−0.24	−1,027,000	−0.11		
Abdominal	Tightened			−1,902,000	−0.22	−1,657,000	−0.19	−1,514,000	−0.17
Skin and cellular	Tightened	−8,938,000	−1.02	−3,227,000	−0.37	−1,936,000	−0.22		
Endocrine	Tightened			−2,189,000	−0.25				
2010									
Elbow	Tightened	−3,017,000	−0.34	−3,852,000	−0.44	−1,666,000	−0.19	−3,249,000	−0.37

NOTE: The numbers in this table represent the expected retirement cost changes associated with each policy change, given the regression estimates of the change in the five-year medical discharge rate, or the percentage of the cohort who have been medically discharged by the end of the fifth YOS. Per-recruit cost estimates are scaled by 10,000. The second number in each pair of rows is the percentage change in cost from the baseline. The model used to generate these estimates assumes that the cost to DoD when the active-component enlistee becomes an officer, becomes a reservist, dies, or separates through a channel other than disability evaluation is 0. Costs of medical retirement, medical separation, and career retirement include the lifetime cash compensation and health care benefits discounted back to the first YOS. We provide a cost estimate only if the relationship between accession medical standards and disability outcomes (the findings from Chapter Three) were significant at the 1- or 5-percent level. Dollar amounts are rounded to the nearest thousand.

accession cohort for each of the three policy-change years. Recall from above that these policy changes went into effect in the middle of these fiscal years, so some accessions in those years joined before the policy change. Therefore, these accession cohort numbers serve the purpose of providing context, but it would be straightforward to multiply the 10,000–service member estimate by the size of a future accession cohort.

A Cost Analysis of Changes to Accession Medical Standards

If people who undergo medical examinations at a MEPS are held to a stricter standard, and are therefore less likely to be medically retired, than the probabilities of leaving the military through all other channels (voluntary separation, career retirement, transfer to the reserves, becoming an officer, death, medical separation, or remaining an active-component enlistee) must increase. We used this concept to develop a notional cost model based on expected postservice cost to DoD for each recruit, which is an average of the postservice benefits paid to exiting service members for each type of exit (e.g., voluntary separation, career retirement) weighted by the probability of that exit. For each change to accession medical standards, we calculated the difference between the baseline expected per-recruit cost to DoD and the adjusted expected cost associated with a change in accession medical policy, because certain types of exits become more or less likely (a likelihood that varies by service and by the policy that changed). Because we did not calculate any costs to agencies outside of DoD and did not calculate or incorporate any current-period or administrative costs, our cost model does not produce a budgetary estimate of the actual cost of the accession medical policy changes, but rather the potential magnitudes of cost differences, in a stylized context.

Because our model does not follow a particular accession cohort over time and rather should be thought of as the per-recruit estimated cost, we scaled our results by 10,000 to give an idea of how small per-recruit savings in the hundreds of dollars could quickly scale, given the large costs associated with medical retirement. Table S.2 summarizes our cost estimates, including the percentage change in baseline costs (for all statistically significant estimates from the previous analysis; four rows did not produce statistically significant results and are therefore excluded from this table). The key message from these results is not the dollar amount but the direction of the cost changes and the relative percentages. Tighter accession standards reduced the expected postservice costs to DoD through a lower probability of medical retirement.

Limitations

The analysis summarized here and detailed further in this report had some limitations. Our analysis of the relationship between accession medical standard policy changes and disability outcomes centered on the date a new policy was issued or revised in DoDI 6130.03 (or its predecessor, DoDI 6130.4).[4] If the new policy was adopted before or after that date, or if supplemental guidance has an important effect on implementation of a new standard, our assignment of service members into pre- or postchange groups might not be accurate.

There are also several data limitations. First, the reason for referral to the disability evaluation system was not available in the data, so we used disability codes assigned at the conclusion of the system to determine whether the condition resulted in a medical discharge. In addition, if the referral condition was available, we could directly analyze the effect of changes in medical retention standards; instead, our analysis was limited to accession medical standards. Second, not all of our disability data sources contained disability ratings for specific conditions,[5] so we characterized the discharge (as either a medical separation or medical retirement) using the overall DoD disability rating. Finally, disability codes were missing altogether for approximately half of Army disability evaluations after 2012. To account for these limitations, we conducted numerous sensitivity analyses and determined that the assignment and data limitations would have minimal effect on our results.

Our cost analysis was not meant to serve as a budgetary estimate of cost savings, but rather a notional model of the magnitude of some of the costs associated with medical discharges. We excluded several costs, such as the cost of replacing and retaining discharged service members and any cost borne by a government agency other than DoD (such as the Department of Veterans Affairs). Our model produced an estimate of the postservice obligations incurred by DoD and a way to show the magnitude of the accession medical policy changes' effect on postservice obligations. In addition, our model reflects current retiree policy and benefit design. If there are changes to the cost, eligibility, or use of TRICARE or the generosity or structure of retiree payments in the future, these estimates would change. Finally, our baseline throughout this report

---

[4] Throughout this report, when we refer to DoDI 6130.03 without a specific date, we mean its current form and its previous iterations:

- DoDI 6130.4, *Criteria and Procedure Requirements for Physical Standards for Appointment, Enlistment, or Induction in the Armed Forces* (Office of the Assistant Secretary of Defense for Health Affairs, 2000, 2004a)
- DoDI 6130.4, *Medical Standards for Appointment, Enlistment, or Induction in the Armed Forces* (OUSD[P&R], 2005a)
- DoDI 6130.03, *Medical Standards for Appointment, Enlistment, or Induction in the Military Services* (OUSD[P&R], 2010c, 2011).

[5] That is, if someone had a 10-percent rating for knee-related pain and a 50-percent rating for lower-back pain, an overall rating of 55 percent (which would be rounded to 60), some data sources would report the rating for each condition (10 percent and 50 percent), but others would report only the combined rating (60 percent), so we could not consistently measure how severe the knee-related condition in question was.

One cannot have a rating of more than 100 percent, so any ratings after the first are entered proportionally, and they are rounded to the nearest 10. For more about this calculation, including examples, see VA, 2018c.

is the effect that accession medical policies have on medical retirements, an estimate we applied to all medical discharges, including separations, in our cost model. Because the cost of medical retirements was higher than that of medical separations and was affected more by changes in accession medical standards, our cost model overstates the costs of medical separations. However, because the cost to DoD of medical separation was trivial compared with the cost of medical retirements, we believe that the impact on our results is minor.

Conclusions and Implications for Future Policy Revisions

Our examination of changes in accession medical standards between 2000 and 2012 showed that, for all but one of the cases (hearing in 2005) in which the standard was tightened, the probability of medical retirement was reduced for at least one military service. The tightening of the hearing standard was correlated with other disability outcomes—in particular, all medical discharges—regardless of rating. However, we did not find a statistically significant increase in the probability of medical retirement for enlistees who were medically evaluated after accession medical standards were relaxed (in the three cases examined). According to our estimates, these policy changes are associated with cost savings to DoD ranging from $1 million to $9 million per 10,000 service members who were accessioned after the policy change.

Our analysis focused on how prior changes to specific accession medical standards affected subsequent medical discharges for service members who enlisted under the new policies. But our model cannot predict how future policy changes would affect disability outcomes and costs for service members who join in the future. That said, findings from our analysis of past policy changes can inform discussions about changes to accession medical standards that might be made in the future. First, we followed service members for up to eight years and found that, although many medical discharges occur very early in a service member's career, we continued to observe these outcomes over the entire period we examined.[6] Additionally, for the three standards we investigated, we found no statistically significant effects on medical retirements when accession medical standards were loosened. For standards that were tightened, we found variation in the effect by the type of the accession medical standard change and by service.

Changes to accession medical standards have important effects, including the ones we measured here: reduced rates of medical discharge when policies are tightened and corresponding cost savings to DoD in the millions of dollars. However, there are also effects that we did not attempt to quantify in this study. Accession medical

---

[6] In alternative specifications, we found that there were no additional measurable impacts past eight years, so the inclusion of longer horizons would not change our findings.

standards are one tool used to screen whether someone can serve in the U.S. military. Unless waivers are granted, tightening standards removes the opportunity to serve for those who do not meet these requirements. Thus, there are trade-offs between recruiting difficulty and the strictness of medical and other standards: The higher the standard to which recruits are held, the more difficult it is to recruit people who meet those standards.

Service stakeholders also indicated that one measure of success is whether a service member completes a first term. Even if a service member is discharged because of a medical condition, that person's service to the military while able to serve has important value, especially if the member is healthy enough to complete a full term of service. Our findings indicate that the decisions to tighten the policies (that we examined) were appropriate, as measured by the effect on downstream disability outcomes, especially in an environment in which much attention is paid to the medical readiness of the force. However, the effects of such policies might be much broader, including some of the trade-offs mentioned above. Further research is needed to understand these additional implications of changes to accession medical standards.

Acknowledgments

This study was originally sponsored by Nancy E. Weaver, then acting principal director for Warrior Care Policy in the Office of the Under Secretary of Defense for Personnel and Readiness (OUSD[P&R]).[1] Her feedback in the early stages of the study helped shape the research questions and study design. James Rodriguez, Deputy Assistant Secretary of Defense for Warrior Care Policy, and Terry Adirim, Deputy Assistant Secretary of Defense for Health Services Policy and Oversight, also in OUSD(P&R), provided invaluable support as the study progressed.

Our action officers served as our main points of contact and ensured that we had access to the resources we needed, including data and information about how policies relevant to the study were evolving. We are grateful to Al Bruner, director of Disability Evaluation Policy; Bret Stevens, director of Disability Evaluation Systems; and Priscilla Berry, director of Disability Evaluation System Operations, all in the office that is now Health Services Policy and Oversight, for their help and insights over the course of the study. In addition, Christopher Arendt of the OUSD(P&R) Office of Military Personnel Policy provided additional action officer support.

The Accession Medical Standards Working Group reviews and recommends changes to accession medical policies—in particular, those contained in the primary U.S. Department of Defense (DoD) instruction we reviewed and used as the basis for analysis in this study. It invited us to present our findings at one of its meetings and offered guidance on additional policies we ought to consider testing. DoD's Disability Advisory Council consists of stakeholders with expertise and policy oversight of the Integrated Disability Evaluation System. They invited us to present at several of the council's quarterly meetings and similarly provided feedback on our findings and offered thoughts on our way forward. We appreciate everything that both groups offered to the study; the research was better for their expertise and guidance.

The research team met with stakeholders from the services and DoD. We met with a team of researchers from the Accession Medical Standards Analysis and Research Activity who provided some background on the research they do in this area

---

[1] Warrior Care Policy no longer exists. The office that sponsored this research is now Health Services Policy and Oversight.

and offered leads on where we might acquire data. To learn about the accession process, and the medical examination more specifically, we visited the Los Angeles Military Entrance Processing Station, where the staff there gave us a tour of what a recruit would experience and offered insights that would help inform our analysis. We value the time and expertise that all of these people offered to improve this research.

This research relied on data from the Defense Manpower Data Center, the services, and DoD. In addition, our cost analysis hinged on data from the DoD Office of the Actuary. Where information we needed was not publicly available, we received tremendous support, including data tailored to our model.

At RAND, Neil Brian Carey and Spencer R. Case helped with an early version of the policy review. Angela Clague provided research assistance. Jill Gurvey, Arthur M. Bullock, and Christine DeMartini provided programming support. Jennie W. Wenger helped with data. Trinidad Beleche and Evan D. Peet contributed to an early version of the cost model. Three Army medical officers who completed the Army Fellows Program at RAND made important contributions to the study: Anthony Marinos, Ann Sims-Columbia, and Joe Penã.

Susan D. Hosek served as a reviewer throughout the course of this study, and her feedback improved it tremendously. Carla Tighe Murray reviewed a draft of this report and provided valuable comments that helped us improve it further.

Abbreviations

ADHD	attention-deficit/hyperactivity disorder
AFI	Air Force instruction
AFQT	Armed Forces Qualification Test
AMSARA	Accession Medical Standards Analysis and Research Activity
AMSWG	Accession Medical Standards Working Group
AR	Army regulation
BMI	body-mass index
CMO	chief medical officer
DES	disability evaluation system
DoD	U.S. Department of Defense
DoDI	Department of Defense instruction
EPTS	existing prior to service
FY	fiscal year
GERD	gastroesophageal reflux disease
IDES	Integrated Disability Evaluation System
JDETS	Joint Disability Evaluation Tracking System
MCO	Marine Corps order
MEB	medical evaluation board
MEPS	military entrance processing station
MERHCF	Medicare-Eligible Retiree Health Care Fund

MilPDS	Military Personnel Data System
MS	musculoskeletal
MTF	medical treatment facility
NAVMED	Navy Bureau of Medicine and Surgery
OACT	Office of the Actuary, U.S. Department of Defense
OUSD(P&R)	Office of the Under Secretary of Defense for Personnel and Readiness
PDBR	Physical Disability Board of Review
PDCAPS	Physical Disability Case Processing System
PEB	physical evaluation board
PTSD	posttraumatic stress disorder
PULHES	physical capacity or stamina, upper extremities, lower extremities, hearing and ears, eyes, and psychiatric
SECNAVINST	Secretary of the Navy instruction
TBI	traumatic brain injury
USMEPCOM	U.S. Military Entrance Processing Command
VA	U.S. Department of Veterans Affairs
VASRD	Veterans Affairs Schedule for Rating Disabilities
VTA	Veterans Tracking Application
YOS	years of service

CHAPTER ONE

Introduction

People who are interested in enlisting in the military must meet certain criteria, including citizenship, education, legal, aptitude, and health. After initial screening with a recruiter, the applicant visits a U.S. Department of Defense (DoD)–operated military entrance processing station (MEPS), where the applicant completes an aptitude exam, the Armed Services Vocational Aptitude Battery; undergoes a medical exam; selects an occupation; and takes the oath of enlistment.

The medical examination portion of the enlistment process consists of six or seven components, depending on gender. A female recruit first takes a pregnancy test; pregnancy is an automatic disqualification from enlistment. The remainder of the exam is standard for all recruits: blood pressure, pulse, audio health, visual health, and a general physical exam (in any order). The final test focuses on orthopedic and neurological concerns. Recruits are also tested for human immunodeficiency virus, drugs, and alcohol (U.S. Military Entrance Processing Command [USMEPCOM], undated). According to the results of the medical examination, the applicant is assigned six scores representing combinations of physical qualification categories: physical capacity or stamina (P), upper extremities (U), lower extremities (L), hearing and ears (H), eyes (E), and psychiatric (S), collectively called PULHES. Scores in each category range from 1 to 4, with 1 indicating no impairment and 4 indicating significant impairment.

DoD has a minimum set of standards for all portions of the screening that takes place at a MEPS, including medical standards. In addition, each branch of the military has its own requirements, which are often identical to but cannot be less restrictive than DoD's. Throughout the course of the study, we learned that DoD policy is the key document at the MEPS exam, so we do not believe that service members were being held to a higher service standard following a DoD change.

Any recruit who does not meet one or more of DoD's medical standards—or the stricter requirement set forth by the service the recruit is joining, if applicable—must receive a waiver for any unmet standard in order to be allowed to enlist. If a waiver is needed, the chief medical officer (CMO) at the MEPS makes that determination, and the request is sent to the waiver authority at the service the recruit is seeking to join.

DoD accession standards are reviewed and revised by the Accession Medical Standards Working Group (AMSWG). The process is governed by the Medical and

Personnel Executive Steering Committee, a group that meets quarterly to provide policy oversight and guidance for setting accession medical standards. The Accession Medical Standards Analysis and Research Activity (AMSARA) provides the Medical and Personnel Executive Steering Committee and AMSWG with evidence-based evaluations of accession medical standards to inform reviews and revisions to the standards (Defense Health Board, 2013; see also AMSARA, 2015, and Walter Reed Army Institute of Research, 2016).

Accession medical standards change over time, and the reasons they change vary. Sometimes, standards are relaxed to help the services meet recruiting targets or because the standard is viewed as too restrictive and unlikely to affect a recruit's ability to serve (see, for example, Vanden Brook, 2017, and Tilghman, 2016). On the other hand, medical standards might be tightened if a certain medical condition is thought to be associated with reduced medical readiness.

The standards to which a recruit is held at the time of the medical examination can have an impact on health over the course of that recruit's career. Day-to-day military duties are physically demanding, and deployments can impose additional physical strain and are often associated with mental health issues as a result of exposure to potentially traumatic events. If service members join at a time when standards are relaxed, they may be, on average, less able to withstand the physical rigor of military service and experience injuries at a higher rate than service members who are held to a higher physical standard. In this study, we measured this relationship by investigating prior changes to specific accession medical standards and the resulting impact on medical discharges for corresponding health conditions. This relationship speaks directly to whether instances in which physical standards are relaxed are subsequently correlated with increases in disability outcomes and whether tighter physical standards are associated with fewer subsequent medical discharges.[1]

The results of this analysis could provide evidence of whether the change in an accession medical standard is appropriate. If we found that relaxed standards were not associated with an increase in the probability of being medically discharged, it would be reasonable to interpret the change in standard as appropriate, at least in terms of this particular outcome. Before the standard was relaxed, accession standards were screening out potential recruits who were not issued waivers but who would be fit to serve, thereby making recruiting unnecessarily difficult. A similar argument can be made for standards that are tightened if service members are less likely to be medically discharged as a result of a policy change. However, the timing of the medical discharge could be an important consideration. The services generally expressed the opinion that getting a full term out of a recruit might be a sufficient return. For conditions that are

---

[1] Throughout this report, we use the word *disabled* or *disability* in reference to a condition identified and rated through the DoD disability evaluation system (DES) or the DoD–U.S. Department of Veterans Affairs (VA) Integrated Disability Evaluation System (IDES).

likely to manifest later in a career, it might not be appropriate to tighten standards in such a way that service members who could have served for a term would be screened out under the new policy.

Existing research on accession medical standards has generally focused on comparing the attrition and medical discharge outcomes of those with and without waivers for a medical condition. There are a few limitations to this approach. First, restricting the analysis to service members with a particular type of health waiver results in small samples and limits the statistical power of the analysis. For example, AMSARA found that more than 70 percent of existing-prior-to-service (EPTS) discharges for asthma were for cases that were concealed, and only 1 percent were waived—a ratio of 70 to 1.[2] Second, changes to accession medical standards affect more than whether a service member needs a waiver to enlist. For example, policy changes can affect whether the condition is disqualifying, the definition of the condition, the method used for detecting a condition, and the critical values for disqualification (e.g., lab values).

In this study, we examined changes to accession medical standards on service member health using downstream medical discharges as our measure. Service members who become wounded, ill, or injured while serving and whose ability to continue to serve is compromised because of the condition or impairment can be referred for disability evaluation. If, during the evaluation, the military department in which the person is serving determines that the service member does not meet medical retention standards, the member is awarded a disability rating and is either medically retired (that is, has a disability rating of 30 percent or more) or medically separated (that is, has a disability rating of less than 30 percent). Someone medically separated with benefits receives a lump-sum severance payment and six months of health care benefits. A service member who is medically retired receives lifetime cash benefits and health care benefits (similar benefits to those who serve for a career, 20 years or more). There are three causes for separation without disability benefits: "the unfitting condition resulted from injury that was due to intentional misconduct or willful neglect; the disability [having been] incurred during a period of unauthorized absence; [or] the disability . . . not [having been] incurred or aggravated in the line of duty" (for example, an EPTS condition) ("Army Integrated Disability Evaluation System [IDES]," undated).

Our analysis was restricted to active-component enlisted service members, and we followed them for up to eight years of service (YOS), depending on when they

---

[2] *EPTS discharges* refers to "illnesses, conditions, and prodromal symptoms" that existed prior to the service member's enlistment in the military (DoDI 1332.38 [Assistant Secretary of Defense for Force Management Policy, 1996). When evaluating a service member for disability, the services presume that preexisting conditions were aggravated by serving in the military, but this presumption can be overcome if the physical evaluation board (PEB) determines that the worsening of the condition followed its "natural progression." The service member can be compensated for a condition that existed prior to service only if the condition was caused by or permanently aggravated as a result of service. See, for instance, "Army Integrated Disability Evaluation System (IDES)," webpage, undated.

were accessioned, recording for each YOS whether the service member was medically discharged.[3] In our analysis file, active-component enlisted personnel represent 79 percent of all initial disability referrals. As we illustrate in Chapter Four, approximately half of all medical discharges occur in the first five YOS.

The balance between defining accession medical standards in such a way to recruit the right pool of talent to serve the needs of the military and ensuring that those who join retain a level of health and fitness that allows them to meet medical requirements and continue to serve is delicate and complex. Because of this, the Office of Warrior Care Policy in the Office of the Secretary of Defense for Personnel and Readiness asked the RAND National Defense Research Institute to examine the relationship between accession medical standards and disability evaluations.[4] Because of the potentially large costs associated with medical discharges, we were also asked to estimate the costs associated with changes to accession medical standards.

Before turning to these questions, we first describe previous research in this area, to place our analysis and findings into context.

A Review of Prior Research on Accession Medical Standards and Disability Separations

As introduced above, the fundamental policy question of this analysis was this: How have changing accession medical standards affected the likelihood of disability separations among the services? The trade-off in changing these accession medical standards is that, although having less strict standards mean that more applicants can be accepted, thereby lowering recruitment costs, this new applicant pool might have, on average, more service members with health conditions that increase the risk that they will become unfit. But this trade-off depends on how selective a particular accession medical standard is. Some standards might screen out applicants who would not have any greater likelihood of being medically discharged than the average service member. Quantifying this trade-off requires measuring the extent to which accepting a marginal applicant has an impact on subsequent disability.

This policy question has been explored previously, primarily by AMSARA, which issues annual reports on both accession standards and the DES. It has also produced a

---

[3] In alternative specifications, we found that there were no additional measurable impacts past eight years, so the inclusion of longer horizons would not change our findings. We express YOS as completed YOS, rather than standard YOS. For example, the first YOS is 1, equivalent to 0 completed YOS. A service member becomes eligible for retirement after 19 completed YOS (the 20th year).

For our multivariate analysis, we followed these service members for either five or eight years; however, for some characteristics, we followed them for other lengths of time.

[4] Warrior Care Policy no longer exists. The office that sponsored this research is now Health Services Policy and Oversight.

range of publications measuring correlations between service members with identified health conditions at accession or during service and the propensity to separate from service, as well as studies comparing accession and service characteristics of service members assigned specific Veterans Affairs Schedule for Rating Disabilities (VASRD) ratings at the time of medical discharge and those without such VASRDs.[5] AMSARA has conducted prospective analyses of service experience by examining an extensive array of conditions for which waivers were granted, including asthma, knee injury, attention-deficit/hyperactivity disorder (ADHD), myopia, hepatitis, sexually transmitted infection, and hearing deficiency (see Clark, Li, et al., 2000; Cox et al., 2000; Camarca and Krauss, 2001; Clark, Howell, et al., 2002; Krauss et al., 2006; Otto et al., 2006; Niebuhr, Li, et al., 2007; and Page et al., 2012). Similarly, it has conducted retrospective analysis on a similarly broad range of health conditions at the time of disability separation, including posttraumatic stress disorder (PTSD), hearing loss, traumatic brain injury (TBI), back-related disability, and asthma (see Niebuhr, Krampf, et al., 2011; Packnett et al., 2012; Gubata, Packnett, Feng, et al., 2013; Gubata, Packnett, and Cowan, 2014; Gubata, Piccirillo, et al., 2014; Elmasry et al., 2017; Piccirillo, Packnet, Boivin, et al., 2015; and Piccirillo, Packnet, Cowan, et al., 2016).

In its prospective, waiver-focused studies, AMSARA employs cohort survival analyses that match a set of service members with waivers for a specific condition with a sample of service members without such waivers, then estimate differences in outcomes (e.g., EPTS discharges, disability separations) at various lengths of time after accession, by the waivered group versus the nonwaivered group. In its retrospective medical discharge studies, AMSARA employs a case-control approach, matching service members who were medically discharged with a particular VASRD or set of VASRDs to otherwise–observationally similar service members who were not discharged with that VASRD or set of VASRDs, and compares characteristics at accession and during service of those who separated with the health condition under consideration and of those who did not.

Both of these methodologies are commonly used in epidemiology and provide correlations of individual characteristics with outcomes of interest. However, these correlations do not necessarily inform the policy question of how *changing* an accession medical standard will affect the outcomes of interest. The disconnect stems from selection over unobservable characteristics. For example, in Clark, Li, et al., 2000, the authors report their comparison of the probability of staying on active duty up to 900 days after accession between 587 service members who received waivers for asthma with 1,761 service members, matched on age, service, sex, accession month, and race, who did not receive waivers. They found no statistically significant differ-

---

[5] A service member who is medically discharged or who files a disability claim with VA after separation from the military is issued a disability rating for the disabling condition(s). Each condition is assigned a VASRD code, and ratings correspond to those codes.

ences in attrition; indeed, there was a slightly *higher* likelihood of staying on active duty among those with waivers for asthma.

Taken at face value, one recommendation from this study might be to loosen the accession medical standard for asthma because accessioning service members with waivers for asthma were just as likely to continue to serve as those who did not. However, this conclusion rests on the assumption that those receiving waivers for asthma are representative of a marginal asthmatic applicant. But the authors also present a breakdown of asthma EPTS discharges by whether they had received waivers: Only 1.2 percent of this group had, while 16.9 percent were not aware that they had asthma, 5.4 percent were known to have asthma but were accessioned without waivers, and 72.8 percent *concealed their asthma*. This breakdown indicates that waivers are a poor measure of the prevalence of service members with particular health conditions. Changing an accession medical standard can change the likelihood that a waiver is granted, the likelihood that a physician requests a waiver for a condition identified, the effort a physician puts into detecting a condition, the likelihood that an applicant reveals a condition, and even potentially the likelihood that someone chooses to apply, especially if recruiters are aware of such medical standard changes. Indeed, in this example, those who reveal their asthma at the MEPS might be disproportionately healthier or more motivated in other dimensions and are thus willing to "take the risk" of being granted waivers, explaining the lack of difference in attrition rates. If asthma and other conditions that can be difficult to detect but straightforward to treat (at least mild cases) are not disqualifying, more recruits might be willing to disclose that they have the condition. With proper treatment, there might not be a difference in readiness between those without the condition and those with the condition who are being treated.

The case-control methodology used in the retrospective medical discharge analyses also provides limited evidence on how policy changes will affect later disability outcomes. For example, for Gubata, Piccirillo, et al., 2014, the authors examined 9,181 Army and 863 Marine Corps back-related medical discharges and compared them with 50,220 enlistees matched on accession year and service. They then compared what characteristics were more prevalent in those with back-related discharges, finding that those with a history of back diagnosis at the MEPS were almost twice as likely to be back-related medical discharges and that enlistees who were overweight or obese at the time of accession were 17 percent and 35 percent more likely to be back-related medical discharges.

However, the linkage between these characteristics at accession and subsequent disability outcomes can be confounded by any unobservable characteristics, such as intrinsic motivation or previous work experience, which can be correlated both with accession variables (such as a history of back problems) and with subsequent disability outcomes. For example, the authors also found that multiple deployments *decrease* the likelihood of back-related disability by more than 40 percent, yet clearly the policy implication is not to deploy service members more in order to lower medical discharges; the underlying relationship is that soldiers and marines who are healthy enough to deploy multiple times are also less likely to have severe back problems.

To infer the effect that a change in accession medical standards has on disability outcomes, we would want variation in the likelihood of acceptance that would be independent of any characteristics except the underlying specific health condition at hand. In Chapter Three, we discuss the issues surrounding the role of unobservable characteristics and selection in receiving a waiver at the time of accession by using historical examples of exactly this variation (previous changes in accession medical standards).

We note here that our focus in this study was the effect that changing these standards has on disability outcomes alone; many other outcomes of direct interest (e.g., deployability, performance) were beyond the scope of this study, largely for data reasons. Our analyses present estimates of one of the costliest outcomes associated with changes in the average health of a service member: medical discharge. By focusing on historical changes, we speak to how changes in accession medical standards are correlated with later disability outcomes for the applicants who were evaluated according to these standards during their accession medical examinations. To isolate the effect that changes to accession medical standards have on medical discharges (separating this effect from other unobservable differences across service members), we focus on accession medical standard changes that we can connect to specific health conditions (measured by the presence of a VASRD code) at the time of medical discharge.

Organization of This Report

Because our analysis examined the effects of changes in accession medical standards, we begin in Chapter Two with an overview of DoD and service accession medical policies and how they have changed over time. Then, in Chapter Three, we describe our methodology and the data used, followed by the findings of our analysis of the relationship between changes in accession medical standards and downstream disability outcomes. Chapter Four presents cost estimates of the changes to accession medical standards that had statistically significant effects on medical discharges. In Chapter Five, we summarize our findings and conclusions.

CHAPTER TWO

Documenting Policy Changes to Inform Statistical Analyses

The starting point for assessing the relationship between accession medical standards and medical discharges is identifying changes in accession medical policies over time. In this chapter, we provide an overview of the medical evaluation process over a service member's career and then describe the documents that guide those decisions. Our analysis evaluated groups of enlistees who underwent medical examinations right before and right after changes in medical accession policies; therefore, we examined the relevant policy documents to determine whether standards were relaxed or made stricter and which conditions were affected. We conclude with a summary of the findings of this review and then describe our analysis of the relationship between the policy changes and disability outcomes.

Overview of the Medical Evaluation Process

The medical standards of DoD and the services are governed by a series of documents that cover accession, waivers, retention, deployability, and disability evaluation:

- Accession medical standards are used primarily by physicians at MEPS to evaluate potential recruits' health and fitness. If an applicant fails to meet accession standards, a waiver must be granted for the applicant to join.
- A waiver is requested by a MEPS physician and sent to the service for a decision. Unlike many of the policies discussed here, waiver decisions are guided by service policy only.
- Medical retention standards are used by military physicians at medical treatment facilities (MTFs) to evaluate medical fitness on an annual or as-needed basis for service members currently serving.
- Deployability standards are used by the unit physician and commanding officer prior to any service member deployment.
- Disability evaluation is conducted by two boards made up of clinicians and personnel management officers who determine whether the service member meets

medical retention standards and, if not, whether the service member is fit for duty.

These stages of medical evaluation and the primary standards used at each stage are represented conceptually in Figure 2.1.[1] In this chapter, we provide a brief overview of each medical evaluation stage.

Figure 2.1
Overview of the Medical Evaluation Process

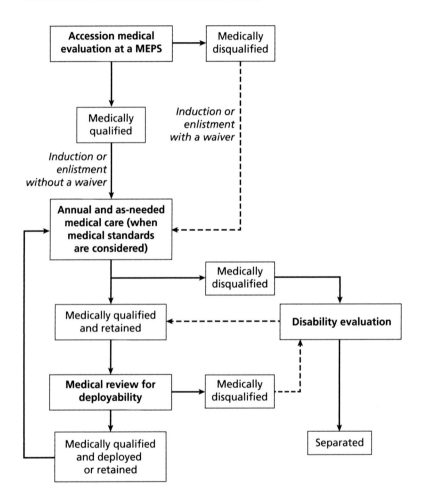

[1]   Additional DoD and service-specific policy documents that govern medical and physical standards can be found in Tables A.1 and A.2, respectively, in Appendix A.

Accession Medical Standards

Accession medical standards are used in the prescreening process at a MEPS,[2] where potential recruits are evaluated for medical qualification to serve. DoDI 6130.03, *Medical Standards for Appointment, Enlistment, or Induction in the Military Services*, is the DoD-level document that governs accession medical standards across the armed forces, including officers and enlisted members in the active and reserve components (Office of the Under Secretary of Defense for Personnel and Readiness [OUSD(P&R)], 2011). Accession medical policy is designed to make sure that people who enter the military can withstand the rigors of training and the physical demands of working in the military. If these medical standards are not met, they are grounds for rejection from military service, or the service has to grant the applicant a medical waiver to serve. DoDI 6130.03 is the foundation for the Army, Navy, Air Force, and Marine Corps service-specific accession medical standards.[3] While DoDI 6130.03 is the primary governing document, if a military service wishes to make a particular medical standard stricter, the service can do so, and the MEPS physician will use that service-specific standard in evaluating the potential recruit. For the policy changes we examined for this study—those for DoDI 6130.03 in 2004, 2005, 2010, and 2011—we reviewed service language. All three services eventually matched DoD policy, but the Army and Air Force took two years to implement DoD's 2004 changes and one and one-half years to implement the 2005 changes. In 2009, the Air Force simply references the DoD instruction (DoDI). The Navy implemented DoD's 2004 and 2005 changes in late 2005. Therefore, we did not find instances in which the service language was stricter than DoD's before the change. The services' lag in implementing DoD changes means that, when DoD standards were relaxed, for a period of time, the service policies were more restrictive until they caught up.

Retention Medical Standards

Retention medical standards are service specific and used in the determination of whether a current service member should be referred to a medical evaluation board (MEB) for consideration for medical discharge. The primary consideration in these standards is whether the service member is medically fit to perform the duties of the member's current job. In some cases, these medical standards might be less restrictive than standards for accession because they are intended for service members who have been in the service for several years and whose job duties might not be as physically demanding.

---

[2] At the time of this writing, there are 65 MEPS in the United States and Puerto Rico: 31 in the Western Sector (west of the Mississippi River plus one in Alaska and one in Hawaii) and 34 in the Eastern Sector (east of the Mississippi River plus the one in Puerto Rico).

[3] Services also have specific medical standards and policies for special communities (e.g., pilots, special operations forces) that sometimes contain stricter medical and physical standards than general service standards. We did not include these standards or policies in our analysis.

Deployability Medical Standards

Deployability medical standards determine whether a service member is "medically able to accomplish [the member's] duties in deployed environments" (OUSD[P&R], 2010b, § 1). These standards apply to any type of deployment outside of the continental United States of more than 30 days in duration, including humanitarian missions and combat operations. Decisions about deployability depend on the kind of deployment environment and the type of job duties that the service member would face.

Waivers

Medical waivers are a mechanism for the services to grant exceptions to potential recruits who do not meet accession medical standards. If a potential recruit is determined to be medically *disqualified*, the CMO at a MEPS can recommend that a waiver be requested. In interviews with subject-matter experts at the Los Angeles MEPS, we learned that there are no DoD-wide standards by which medical waivers are judged.[4] Each case is reviewed individually by the CMO at a MEPS, who then sends a request for a waiver to the service waiver authority.[5] Although there are no written standards, it is typical for CMOs to request waivers for conditions they know have been waived in the past. Within our analytic sample, the percentage of accessioning service members with nonheight, nonweight medical waivers range from just over 1.5 percent to just under 4 percent, depending on the service and year, as discussed in greater detail in Chapter Three.

Disability Evaluation

A service member who becomes wounded, ill, or injured while serving and, after a period of treatment, is deemed by a treating provider to be unfit to continue serving can be referred to the Integrated DES (IDES), a system run jointly by DoD and VA. Prior to 2007, when IDES was initially rolled out, the two departments evaluated each service member separately. Our analysis covers both periods (pre-2007 IDES rollout,

---

[4] Throughout the course of the study, the research team met with and briefed stakeholders from the services and DoD, including AMSWG, the Disability Advisory Council, and AMSARA and individuals who manage data, oversee the disability evaluation process in the services, or are concerned with recruiting and accession medical policies. The team also visited the Los Angeles MEPS to learn what happens when a recruit visits. The research was approved by RAND's Human Subjects Protection Committee (protocol 2015-0417) and by the Defense Health Agency's Human Research Protection Program (component designated official [CDO] 15-2027).

[5] For recruits to the Army, waiver requests go to U.S. Army Recruiting Command. For recruits to the National Guard, waiver requests go first to the state, then to the National Guard Bureau Joint Surgeon's Office. For recruits to the U.S. Navy, waiver requests go to the commander, Navy Recruiting Command (N33) section in the Navy Bureau of Medicine and Surgery. For recruits to the Marine Corps, waiver requests go through the chief of the Navy Bureau of Medicine and Surgery, who makes recommendations to the commanding general, Marine Corps Recruiting Command, the waiver authority. For recruits to the Air Force, waiver requests go to the Air Force Surgeon General. We obtained the information in this footnote from a visit to the Los Angeles MEPS, April 27, 2016.

as IDES was being adopted across DoD through fiscal year [FY] 2011, through full implementation), so throughout this report, we refer to the system as the DES.

A disability evaluation consists of three phases. The first, the MEB's assessment, is conducted at the MTF and determines whether the service member meets medical retention standards. Early in this phase, VA conducts a comprehensive physical exam of the service member, recording all conditions identified by the physician or claimed by the service member. The MEB, made up of clinicians and personnel management officers, uses information from the exam to decide whether the service member meets medical retention standards. If these standards are met, the service member is returned to duty.

If the service member is found to not meet medical retention standards, the case is forwarded to the PEB. Unlike the MEBs, which are based at MTFs, PEBs are centralized within the military services.[6] The PEB determines whether the conditions found by the MEB make the service member unfit for duty, taking into consideration the service member's duty assignment, severity of the condition, and other factors. If the service member is considered fit for duty, the service member is returned to duty. If the PEB determines that the service member is not fit for duty, the case is forwarded to VA, where each condition is assigned a VASRD code and a corresponding disability rating. The individual condition ratings are combined to form two overall ratings, one by DoD, which accounts for only unfitting conditions, and one by VA, which includes all conditions. The PEB also determines the service member's eligibility for benefits, which depends on whether the impairment occurred as a result of intentional conduct or willful neglect, happened during a period of unauthorized absence, or was incurred or aggravated outside the line of duty.

The fitness determination and DoD rating determine the service member's final disposition. Service members whose DoD combined ratings for all conditions making them unfit are less than 30 percent are medically separated. In general, a medically separated service member receives a one-time lump-sum severance payment and health care benefits for 180 days following separation. Service members who are assigned a disability rating of 30 percent or higher are considered medically retired, and they receive monthly cash payments and health care for life. If the medical condition is considered stable, the service member can be placed on the Permanent Disability Retired List. If the medical condition is not yet stabilized or if the service member has certain conditions that require it (such as PTSD), the service member can be placed on the Temporary Disability Retired List. A service member placed on the Temporary Disability Retired List can be reevaluated for up to five years until a permanent disposition

---

[6] At the time of this writing, the Army had three PEBs, and the Air Force and Navy (handling evaluations for both the Navy and the Marine Corps) each had one.

is determined.[7] Medical retirements represent approximately two-thirds of all medical discharges; the remaining one-third are medical separations.

Service members who are medically retired or separated then enter the final phase of IDES, the transition. This is largely an administrative phase during which out-processing occurs and service members use any accumulated leave. The transition phase concludes with discharge from the military, and the first disability payment arrives within 30 days of discharge. The entire evaluation, including transition and the 30 days before the first payment arrives, is supposed to take no more than 295 days for active-component service members.[8]

At various points throughout the evaluation, the service member makes decisions about concurring with the findings of the MEB or PEB or requesting an appeal. The service member also has access to legal counsel. Finally, IDES was introduced as a joint program between DoD and VA in 2007. Prior to 2007, the two departments ran separate disability evaluations, often resulting in two sets of identified conditions and different ratings for the same condition. The key decisions and service member dispositions between DoD's legacy DES and the post-2007 IDES are similar, including referral to the MEB, the MEB's assessment of medical retention, the PEB's decision on fitness to serve, medical retirement and separation dispositions, and receipt of DoD disability rating for unfitting conditions.

Policy Review: Scope, Methodology, and Findings

Although there are many points at which medical evaluation occurs, we limited our analysis to accession medical standards.[9] In particular, we examined disability outcomes among service members who joined right before and right after a change in standards.[10]

---

[7]   Between the time we wrote this report and the time it was published, the policy changed to three years.

[8]   Between the time we wrote this report and the time it was published, the policy changed to 250 days.

[9]   Currently, medical retention standards do not exist at the DoD level—only for individual medical services. However, at the time of this writing, the Office of the Deputy Assistant Secretary of Defense for Health Services Policy and Oversight is working with stakeholders to develop universal medical retention standards. This is a similar approach to AMSWG's development of the accession medical standards analyzed in this study.

It would be possible to analyze the effect that changes in service-specific medical retention standards have on downstream disability outcomes, but the way retention standards affect disability is through the referral process. Electronic data on the condition for which a service member is referred to the DES is not available, nor is referral date under the legacy DES, so there would be no way to link a particular change in medical retention standards to patterns in referrals for that condition. Implicitly, our estimates capture the effects of changes in retention standards because they affect whether a service member is referred for disability evaluation, but we cannot isolate the effect from the effect of changes in accession standards.

[10] Each analysis included four years of accessions—roughly two years of accessions before the policy change and two after. For instance, our analysis of the January 2005 change in the DoDI defined the preaccession

Scope

Our policy review covered changes to accession medical standards between FYs 2000 and 2012. We scoped the policy review to these years to align with our data analysis that we discuss in more detail in Chapter Three. The specific policies covered in this review include the following:

- **DoD: DoDI 6130.03, Medical Standards for Appointment, Enlistment, or Induction in the Military Services.**[11] This instruction standardizes physical and medical requirements for appointment, enlistment, or induction of service personnel to eliminate inequities based on race, sex, or location of examination. Precise definitions are provided for conditions that cause separation or assignment limitation. This DoDI was issued or updated five times during the study period, in 2000, 2004, 2005, 2010, and 2011. This instruction served as our principal focus for the policy review.
- **Army: Army Regulation (AR) 40-501, Medical Services: Standards of Medical Fitness** (Headquarters, Department of the Army, 2017b). This regulation implements DoDI 6130.03 and provides information on medical fitness standards for accession and retention. The document also clarifies medical examination requirements and details physical profiling authority of physicians. AR 40-501 was issued 15 times during the study period (Headquarters, Department of the Army, 2002a, 2002b, 2003, 2004a, 2004b, 2004c, 2005, 2006a, 2006b, 2007a, 2007b, 2007c, 2008, 2010, 2011).
- **Air Force: Air Force Instruction (AFI) 48-123, Medical Examinations and Standards** (Director of Medical Operations and Research, 2018). This instruction implements DoDI 6130.03 and provides guidance on medical examinations and standards for accession and retention in the Air Force. It identifies medical conditions requiring attention and assists with the evaluation of disability claims. This instruction was issued four times during the study period, in 2000, 2001,

---

policy change group as those service members who accessed in FYs 2003 and 2004 and the first three months of FY 2005 and the postaccession policy change group as those service members who were accessioned in the rest of FY 2005 and in FY 2006. We excluded those whose medical exams occurred within 30 days before or after the date the DoDI was issued.

[11] Throughout this report, when we refer to DoDI 6130.03 without a specific date, we mean its current form and its previous iterations:

- DoDI 6130.4, *Criteria and Procedure Requirements for Physical Standards for Appointment, Enlistment, or Induction in the Armed Forces* (Office of the Assistant Secretary of Defense for Health Affairs, 2000, 2004a)
- DoDI 6130.4, *Medical Standards for Appointment, Enlistment, or Induction in the Armed Forces* (OUSD[P&R], 2005b)
- DoDI 6130.03, *Medical Standards for Appointment, Enlistment, or Induction in the Military Services* (OUSD[P&R], 2010c, 2011).

2006, and 2009 (Office of the Command Surgeon, 2000, 2001, 2006; Office of the Chief of Aerospace Medicine Policy and Operations, 2009).

• **Navy and Marine Corps: Navy Bureau of Medicine and Surgery (NAVMED) P-117, Manual of the Medical Department (MANMED)** (NAVMED, 2018a). This manual details physical examination requirements and standards for enlistment, commission, and special duty for the Navy and Marine Corps. This manual was issued twice during the study period, in 2001 and 2005 (NAVMED, 2001, 2005).

We collected policy documents (those listed above and others that we referenced in our policy review) through internet searches, stakeholder interviews with military medical subject-matter experts, and archived document requests from the Defense Technical Information Center, Defense Health Headquarters, the Pentagon Library, the U.S. Army Publishing Directorate, the U.S. Army Heritage and Education Center, the U.S. Army War College, the U.S Air Force Publishing Directorate, and the Navy's Bureau of Medicine and Surgery.

Methodology

Once all the documents were collected, we extracted the document text to Excel and Word to organize the content in tables by policy revision date and body system category.[12] We then compared the text changes (added, deleted, or otherwise altered text) in each body system category across the policy documents. Changes were then classified as "tightening," "loosening," or "no change."[13] Additional details about the methodology are included in Appendix A. General enlistment standards across the service components mirror those outlined in DoDI 6130.03. Sometimes there is a lag in updating the service-specific policy, which we believe to be due to processing delays, not intentional decisions to retain old standards. For example, after the 2005 reissuance of DoDI 6130.03, AR 40-501 was still consistent with 2004 standards until June 2006, when the language was updated to match the 2005 DoDI language.

---

[12] We used the condition category structure used in DoDI 6130.03 to organize the content and enable comparison across the different policy documents. During the years of our study period, these categories remained largely the same. However, it is important to note that conditions sometimes changed categories. For example, sleep disorders did not have their own category until 2010; prior to 2010, sleep disorders were scattered across other categories, such as "infectious diseases" and "other behavioral problems."

[13] When we began this task, we attempted to categorize the magnitude and direction of policy changes with the intent to distinguish between major and minor tightenings and major and minor loosenings at the body system category level. Making this distinction proved to be challenging at the individual condition level, let alone rolling up changes to the body system category level. In many cases, policy changes within a particular body system category were in opposite directions (i.e., both tightening and loosening of standards), and it was not clear which change would dominate. Therefore, we categorize changes only by the direction of the change at the individual condition level.

To correlate medical standard changes to the data analysis piece of this study, we mapped the VASRD codes to body system categories and, when possible, specifically to a condition listed in a body system category, using our own medical subject-matter expertise.[14] In some cases, health conditions might have several VASRD codes. For example, a gastrointestinal bleed was mapped to ten VASRD codes. And in some cases, there was no match of a condition to a VASRD code. For example, metabolic syndromes, such as obesity and dyslipidemia, did not directly map to VASRD codes. The detailed VASRD mapping can be found in Appendix B.[15]

We then used these mappings to quantitatively examine the relationship between medical screening at accession and subsequent medical discharge. Chapter Three details our methodology for the statistical analysis. Taking into account statistical power, we analyzed only those VASRDs for which we had a sufficiently large enough sample (i.e., medical discharges) to be able to detect an effect (should there be an effect to detect). Table 2.1 shows the candidate disability separation conditions for statistical analysis and their corresponding body system categories. This table presents the conditions for which the percentage of disability separations for accession cohorts were at least 1 percent, our threshold for determining the availability of a sufficient number of observations for analysis.

Findings

Generally, we found four types of changes to policy documents: (1) adding disqualifying conditions, (2) changing criteria for which a disqualifying condition is judged (e.g., range-of-motion change, orthotics removed from pes planus), (3) completely removing a standard or disqualifying condition from a standard (e.g., tattoos), and (4) minor wording changes that appear to intend to clarify the standard but do not change the nature of the standard.

We empirically analyzed (as described in the following chapters) only those VASRDs represented in at least 1 percent of medical discharges to potentially detect an effect of a 0.01-percentage-point policy change on disability outcomes at a statistical power of 0.8. Table 2.2 details our interpretations of the changes to policy for those conditions. We observed the largest number of changes to the standards in 2005 and

---

[14] An active-duty military officer (a physician's assistant) and RAND staff member trained as a physician evaluated the policy changes and mapped them to corresponding VASRD codes.

[15] The National Defense Authorization Act for FY 2008 (Pub. L. 110-181, 2008) directed DoD to establish the Physical Disability Board of Review (PDBR), which reviews, at the veteran's request, medical separations that occurred between September 11, 2001, and December 31, 2009. The goal is to ensure that cases were adjudicated fairly and accurately. The PDBR uses medical information provided by VA and the military department to make a recommendation to the secretary of the military department about whether the veteran's final disposition should remain the same or whether it should be changed to a medical retirement. We did not observe the outcomes of the PDBR; disability outcomes in each person-year reflect the result of the initial evaluation.

Table 2.1
Medical Discharge Conditions for Statistical Analysis

Body System Category	Disability Separation Condition
Abdominal organs and gastrointestinal system	Abdominal organs and gastrointestinal systems
Ears	Ears
Endocrine and metabolic	Endocrine and metabolic system
Learning, psychiatric, and behavioral	Learning, psychiatric, and behavioral
	Mental disorders
Lower extremities	Ankle and foot
	Joint inflammation
	Knee
	Leg (fibula and tibia)
	Tendon inflammation
	Thigh (femur)
Lungs and chest	Asthma
Miscellaneous conditions of the extremities	Ankle and foot
	Joint inflammation
	Leg (fibula and tibia)
	Neurologic: Miscellaneous lower extremity
	Tendon inflammation
Neurologic	Neurologic: Brain disorders, inflammation, and spinal cord
	Neurologic: Epilepsy (brain disorder)
	Neurologic: Miscellaneous lower extremity
Rheumatologic	Rheumatologic
Skin and cellular tissues	Skin and cellular tissues
Sleep disorders	Sleep disorders
Spine and sacroiliac joints	Spine and sacroiliac joints
Systemic	Rheumatologic
Upper extremities	Arm (humerus)
	Hand and wrist
	Joint inflammation
	Tendon inflammation

Table 2.2
Policy Changes Included in Our Analyses

Year	System	Our Name for the System	Policy Change	Direction of Change[a]
2004	Abdominal organs and gastrointestinal system	Abdominal	Added "E1.1.4. Gastrointestinal Bleeding. History of such, unless the cause shall have been corrected and is not otherwise disqualifying (578)" as a disqualifying condition and additions to the hernia standard (E1.1.8.1) "and other abdominal (553), except for small, or asymptomatic umbilical or hiatal."	Tighten
	Lungs and chest	Asthma	Changed the criterion for asthma from "reliably diagnosed at any age" to "reliably diagnosed and symptomatic after the 13th birthday." In case of a doubtful diagnosis of asthma, the requirement for a reversible airflow-obstruction test was removed.	Loosen
2005	Lower extremities	Knee	Changed the criteria for knee range of motion from "E1.8.1.2.1. Full extension, compared with contralateral" and "E1.8.1.2.2. Flexion to 90 degrees" (from the 2004 version) to "E 1.17.1.2.1. Full extension to 0 degrees" and "E 1.17.1.2.2. Flexion to 110 degrees," respectively. Added current medial and lateral collateral ligament injuries and current meniscal injuries as disqualifying conditions.[b]	Tighten
	Abdominal organs and gastrointestinal system	Abdominal	Added to and changed the criteria for certain conditions, such as GERD, airway disease, peptic ulcers, inflammatory bowel diseases, lactase deficiency, metabolic liver disease, and abdominal surgery and obesity surgery.	Tighten
			Deleted congenital abnormality of the stomach or duodenum as a disqualifying condition. Changed the criteria for gastritis, cholecystitis, and splenectomy.	Loosen
	Hearing	Hearing	Changed the criterion for audiometric hearing thresholds from "both ears" to "either ear." Added the use of hearing aids as a disqualifying condition.	Tighten
	Skin and cellular tissue	Skin and cellular	Changed the psoriasis standard from (in 2004) allowing mild cases of psoriasis ("E1.31.17. Psoriasis [696.1]. Unless mild by degree, not involving nail-pitting, and not interfering with the wearing of military equipment or clothing") to "El.20.14. Current or history of psoriasis (696.1) is disqualifying." Added "current or history of" to several conditions, including atopic and contact dermatitis, keloid formation, bullous dermatoses, hyperhidrosis of hands and feet, neurofibromatosis, radiodermatitis, and scleroderma. Added language regarding scars that interfere with satisfactory performance or wearing of military clothing.	Tighten
	Endocrine	Endocrine	Added "current or history of" to several conditions, including adrenal function, diabetes mellitus, hyperthyroidism, and acromegaly. Added pituitary dysfunction as a disqualifying condition.	Tighten

Table 2.2—Continued

Year	System	Our Name for the System	Policy Change	Direction of Change[a]
2010	Upper extremities	Elbow	Changed the criterion for range of motion for the elbow from "El.16.1.2.1. Flexion to 100 degrees" (from 2005) to "Flexion to 130 degrees."	Tighten
	Skin and cellular tissue	Skin and cellular	Changed the standard for atopic dermatitis from "El.20.2. Current or history of atopic dermatitis (691) or eczema (692) after the 9th birthday is disqualifying" in 2005 to "b. Current or history of atopic dermatitis (691) or eczema (692.9) after the 12th birthday."	Loosen
	Lower extremities	Orthotics	Changed the reference to orthotics from "El.17.2.4. Current symptomatic pes planus [acquired (734), congenital (754.6)] or history of pes planus corrected by prescription or custom orthotics is disqualifying" (from 2005) to "(6) Rigid or symptomatic pes planus (acquired (734) or congenital (754.61)" (i.e., pes planus was no longer referred to as disqualifying).	Loosen

NOTE: GERD = gastroesophageal reflux disease.

[a] This column contains our interpretation of whether the policy change loosens or tightens standards.

[b] Several changes were made to the lower-extremities body system category in 2005; we highlight here a few changes pertaining to the knee.

2010. Table A.3 in Appendix A contains descriptions of policy changes across a broader set of body system categories.

We now turn to our analysis of these policy changes. For each of the ten changes identified here, we followed groups of active-component enlisted service members over time to see whether the probability of being medically discharged differed after a policy change. Chapter Three describes our methodology of assessing the relationship between changes to accession medical standards and downstream medical discharges, the analytic file used to conduct the analysis, and our findings.

Analysis of Accession Medical Standard Changes and Medical Discharges

To examine the relationship between the changes to accession medical standards identified in Chapter Two and downstream disability outcomes, we looked at service members who were accessioned right before and right after a policy change and followed them over time to see whether one group had a higher rate of medical discharge than the other. Because accession medical standards apply at the time of physical exam, strictly speaking, we compared service members whose physical exams were conducted before and after these changes in accession standards, irrespective of when the service member entered basic training.

Our basic hypothesis is that, whether a relationship exists between accession medical standards and disability outcomes, service members who are accessioned right after a standard is tightened (or loosened) will be medically discharged at lower (or higher) rates than service members who were accessioned before the policy was tightened (or loosened). However, if there were no measurable change in disabling health conditions after the change in an accession medical standard, our analysis would find no impact of a change in that standard on disability outcomes. Our analysis included the effect of any changes in MEPS screening due to implementation as well; if a tightening standard leads physicians to screen with greater scrutiny, we included such increases in detection and subsequent changes in the health of accessioning service members. In this chapter, we first describe our methodology in more detail, then turn to the data and a summary of our results.

Methodology

Our analysis followed the cohort-based approach of Mastrobuoni, 2009, in that we directly estimated the differences across accession cohorts in the likelihood of being medically discharged with the disabling conditions under analysis during each YOS. After controlling for a rich set of covariates, some constant over time and others, such as age, months of service, and deployment experiences, variable, the remaining differences in medical discharges that had VASRDs corresponding to a standard could be attributed to the change in that standard.

This interpretation would be invalid if potential applicants "sorted" around pending changes in accession medical policy by timing their accession physicals before a tightening or after a loosening or if these accession medical policies were driven by projected future applicant health. Applicants might indeed sort around anticipated changes in accession medical policy if a recruiter knew which changes were coming and could identify motivated recruits who were eligible under the current standards but might not meet new requirements. This is more likely to happen during challenging recruiting environments but is probably not a widespread practice, and we did not expect it to affect our results. To help correct for such occurrences, however, we excluded service members whose medical exams occurred within 30 days of a change to an accession medical standard.

Our approach also rested on the assumption that changes to accession medical standards were not made to compensate for changes in the health of future applicants. This might not always be true. For instance, the prevalence of ADHD and asthma in the general population were both increasing over time, so accession medical standards were changed, allowing those with less-severe illness to qualify for military service.

If applicants were to time their medical exams around expected changes in accession medical standards or if policies were to reflect expected changes in the health of future accession cohorts, our estimates would be biased toward 0, and the findings reported would underestimate the effects that changes to accession medical standards have on medical discharge. For example, violating this assumption means that service members who were accessioned after a standard has tightened would be, on average, less healthy, and we would expect any effect of stronger screening to be combined with a greater underlying rate of disability.

Our control group ($A_i = 0$) was defined as service members whose physical exams, during which accession medical standards are applied, occurred before one of the accession medical standard changes, and our treatment group ($A_i = 1$) includes service members whose physical exams took place after the change in that accession medical standard. Therefore, we estimated the following equation:

$$VASRDDis_{it} = \alpha + \left(\delta_1 + \beta_1 1(A_i = 1)\right) Months_{it} + \left(\delta_2 + \beta_2 1(A_i = 1)\right) Months_{it}^2$$
$$+ \left(\delta_3 + \beta_3 1(A_i = 1)\right) Months_{it}^3 + \Gamma X_{it} + \gamma_t + \varepsilon_{it}.$$

The outcome variable is whether service member i was medically discharged with any of the VASRD codes corresponding to the condition of interest (for that policy change) in FY t.[1] Multiple VASRD codes can exist for a single condition, depending on severity. In our primary specification, we included medical discharges with a combined

---

[1]   Table B.1 in Appendix B contains a full list of which VASRDs were mapped to each policy change that we identified in Chapter Two and tested in this analysis.

DoD rating of at least 30 percent; in alternative analyses reported in Appendix E, we report our estimate of the impact on all medical discharges, regardless of the level of the combined DoD rating, as well as the effect on medical discharges with combined DoD ratings of less than 30 percent.[2]

We chose disability ratings of 30 percent or higher as our baseline specification for several reasons. First, for the cost analysis that we report in Chapter Four, we used estimates from the Office of the Actuary (OACT) indicating the percentage of service members who are medically discharged in each YOS. OACT presents medical retirement rates, but medical separations are grouped with other withdrawals from service, such as voluntary withdrawals at the end of a term of service. We used other data to help isolate medical separations in our cost model, but, to best match the data across analyses, we focused on medical retirements here. Second, as shown in Appendix E, when we looked across all medical discharges (regardless of disability rating), we see that medical retirements drive the results (as a reminder, they represent two-thirds of all medical discharges in our analysis file). The policy effects for medical separations are much smaller and rarely statistically significant.

Next, because legacy disability data do not consistently report disability ratings for each unfitting condition, we were forced to rely on the overall DoD disability rating, which masks the severity of the condition we were examining. By focusing our analysis on the discharges with the higher disability ratings, we hoped that our analysis would do a better job of measuring only the outcomes that were severe enough to warrant discharge. Of course, the condition we were examining might have only a 10-percent disability rating while the retirement outcome was driven by another condition with a much higher rating, but, overall, our dependent variable represented the service members with the most-disabling conditions who probably could not have continued serving even with a low rating on the condition in question.

For service members not medically discharged, the $Months_{it}$ variable is the number of months of service at the end of the given FY; for those medically discharged, it is the number at the time of discharge.[3] The coefficients of interest are the

---

[2] Although we would have preferred to measure the rating for the conditions of interest instead of the combined rating, data limitations prior to the introduction of IDES allowed us to observe only the combined DoD rating.

[3] Months of service enters directly both as a squared term and as a cubic term, to capture flexible nonlinearities in the relationship between length of service and disability outcomes. We included the possibility for nonlinearities in order to avoid imposing assumptions about when medical discharges manifest. For example, if an accession medical standard change screened out health conditions that would result in immediate medical discharge, we would observe this effect as occurring immediately, with no additional marginal effect as months of service continued. A medical standard change that screened out conditions that manifest only later, and hence would not have any effect until years into service, would be estimated as having an effect, but only at a later horizon of service. Our analytic approach thus allowed us to estimate effects flexibly across lengths of service ranging from just after accession to eight YOS. We experimented with different specifications for months of service, and our results were robust.

βs,[4] which estimate how those being accessioned after the accession medical standard change of interest vary in their likelihood of being medically discharged with the corresponding health condition. By including these coefficients as interactions with the months-of-service terms, we measured separate effects by length of service. The X_{it} vector contains individual demographic and service characteristics and is described in the "Data" section below. Finally, γ_t controls for the current FY, accounting for service-wide shocks in a given FY. We present findings from fitting a linear probability model, as written above.[5]

We estimated this equation separately for each service, accession medical standard change, and corresponding health condition. We report five- and eight-year estimates for each condition, for each service. Medical discharge occurs after a period of treatment (generally up to one year for a single condition) and then approximately a one-year disability evaluation, so five- and eight-year estimates really capture injuries and illnesses that present within the first three and six YOS, respectively.

Additionally, although we controlled for changes in retention standards by including variables for each FY separately, as well as a variable in Army analyses following a substantial change in Army retention policies during the middle of FY 2009, our ability to directly test the impact that changes in retention standards have on disability referrals was limited because of a lack of data on referral conditions themselves, as discussed further at the end of the "Data" section.

We did not directly include accession-related measures of health, such as PULHES scores or waivers, in this equation because these indicators are themselves related to our policy change. The concern is that these measures will also be affected by the change in the accession medical standard, and including them would therefore lessen the estimated impact of the medical change itself. That is, service members who require a waiver in a stricter accession medical standard regime differ from those who require a waiver in a looser regime *because of the accession standards themselves.* Hence, including waiver status would incorporate some of the effect of the policy change because we might observe a specific health condition as the result of a waiver granted in a strict accession medical–standard environment, but an identical service member with an

---

[4] We applied two-tailed tests of statistical significance, allowing for the possibility of both increases and decreases in the effect that a particular accession medical standard change has on medical discharges for corresponding health conditions. We took this more conservative statistical approach in order to allow the data to inform our inference as to the accession medical–standard change's effect. For example, it might seem straightforward that a tightening of the standard related to knee flexibility would lead to service members with more-flexible knees being accessioned. However, if applicants who do not satisfy the new knee standard apply for waivers, and waiver authorities therefore tend to approve more knee waivers (because of the large influx of relatively flexible applicants into the waiver applicant pool), average knee health could fall because of this "demand-side" response to accession medical standard changes. Although we did not think that such narratives were likely, we preferred to use a higher standard of statistical significance.

[5] As a sensitivity analysis, not reported here but available from authors upon request, we conducted logit and probit specifications and found quantitatively similar estimates for all reported results.

identical health condition might not require a waiver once that standard is loosened, preventing direct comparison of downstream disability outcomes because we could not observe this condition in those without waivers.

Something similar could happen with PULHES scores. If, under looser standards, more recruits are permitted to join with certain medical conditions, the number of people with PULHES scores greater than 1 (indicating an impairment) would likely increase. If these service members are more likely to be medically discharged, it would appear that there is an association between PULHES scores and disability outcomes, when, in reality, the increased level of higher PULHES scores can be attributed to the relaxed policy. By controlling for these PULHES scores or waivers, we would be measuring the impact that accession standards have only on those members who did not reveal their condition, had these conditions detected, or were judged to require a waiver by the MEPS physician. How these behaviors change after a change in accession medical standards is an important question, but the overall effect of the policy includes disability outcomes for those now accepted, even if the condition was subsequently waivered or otherwise measurably recognized.[6]

Data

To conduct this analysis, we built a person-year file using administrative personnel and disability data. From the Defense Manpower Data Center, we merged data at the time of accession (USMEPCOM data) and during service (the Active Duty Master File, the Work Experience File, and, for the Global War on Terrorism, the Contingency Tracking System). Our dependent variable derives from disability evaluation data, including Veterans Tracking Application (VTA) data and service data containing information on medical discharges (for the Army, the Physical Disability Case Processing System [PDCAPS]; for the Navy and Marine Corps, the Joint Disability Evaluation Tracking System [JDETS]; and, for the Air Force, the Military Personnel Data System [MilPDS]). Our sample includes service members being accessioned from the beginning of FY 2002 through FY 2011.[7] We selected this sample window to ensure

---

[6] An alternative approach would be to conduct an instrumental-variable analysis of the impact that accession standards have on the influx of waivered conditions. However, waiver policy implementation is idiosyncratic in our data, and the number of service members with waivers corresponding to each accession medical standard change is a very small fraction of each group of service members, which limits statistical power.

[7] We defined our comparative groups of service members based on when their medical exams occurred, but, for the purposes of building our analytic file, we did use accession date to define whom we included. Some service members who were accessioned in FY 2002 had their medical exams done in FY 2001. None of the service members included in our analysis had FY 2001 medical exams, so we did not lose anything by not capturing the exam dates of all FY 2002 accessions.

Because of the limited availability of data—in particular, deployment data—our analytic file begins with cohorts who were accessioned after September 11, 2001 (i.e., FY 2002). DoDI 6130.03 was revised in 2000,

that we had enough years to observe a service member through their term of service while also capturing recent policy changes.

The Defense Manpower Data Center's USMEPCOM data allow us to observe not just accessions during our sample window but also applications that did not result in accession. We were also able to observe and link an applicant to that applicant's previous applications. Although we did not specifically study multiple-application patterns, these within-applicant linkages ensure that the accession medical standard used to evaluate that service member is the one that corresponds to the member's most recent physical before accession. It is this most recent physical exam prior to accession that defines whether a service member belongs in the pre– or post–policy change group for the purposes of the regression design described above.

We followed each service member from the time of accession through eight YOS or their discharge, whichever occurred first.[8] Service members who were accessioned more recently cannot be observed for eight full years, so we followed them until our data end. We created a separate observation for each service member for each FY, including individual characteristics, deployment experiences, and an indicator for whether the service member was medically discharged in that FY. The full list of variables we use in our analysis are as follows:

- individual and demographic characteristics: sex, age, race and ethnicity (non-Hispanic white, non-Hispanic black, non-Hispanic other race, and Hispanic), marital status (currently married or not), education (less than high school, high school, and more than high school), Armed Forces Qualification Test (AFQT) category (I, II, IIIA, IIIB, and IVA through V), and body-mass index (BMI)
- service characteristics: months of service, pay grade, and standardized occupation
- MEPS information: Western versus Eastern Sector, MEPS identifier
- deployments: whether ever deployed, deployed three years ago, cumulative years of deployment as of three years ago, and the number of deployments as of three years ago.

Lagged deployment variables warrant an explanation. If a service member seeks treatment for a condition that impairs the ability to do the member's job, treatment could be ongoing for a period of time before the service member is referred to the MEB.[9] Then, once the member is referred, the evaluation is supposed to be com-

---

2004, 2005, 2010, and 2011. To test changes to 2004, we compared the 2004 and 2000 versions. Therefore, our policy review began with 2000, but our analytic file and data analysis began with service members who were accessioned in FY 2002.

[8]   In alternative specifications, we found that there were no additional measurable impacts past eight years, so the inclusion of longer horizons would not change our findings.

[9]   The services have different policies for how long treatment can take place. The Army treats the soldier until the impairment has stabilized, the course of recovery is relatively predictable, and additional treatment will not

pleted within 265 days (from referral to discharge). That means for approximately two years, sometimes longer, the service member is undergoing treatment and evaluation for a potentially unfitting condition and, importantly, is not deploying. If the service member has deployed within the previous two years, medical discharge will not yet have happened. Therefore, in considering the time of medical discharge, we controlled for deployments that occurred three or more years ago.

Appendix C contains descriptive statistics for the samples used in our analyses of the 2004 and 2005 changes to accession medical standards, as well as regression coefficients for a sample of policy changes.

Variation in the Health of New Accessions

Figures 3.1 and 3.2 show the overall number of applicants and accessions in each FY. As Figure 3.1 shows, all of the services experienced a gradual decline in the number of applications over the years studied. Although the proportional decline is at least 20 percent across all services from 2002 to 2011, it is highest for the Army, which experienced a decline in applications of nearly 40 percent—corresponding to nearly 100,000 fewer applicants in FY 2011 than in FY 2002.

Despite the decline in the number of applicants, the overall number of *accessions* is relatively unchanged during this period, as Figure 3.2 illustrates, although there is some year-to-year variation. To maintain relatively constant numbers of accessions, these services are necessarily less selective by FY 2011 than they were in FY 2002, inasmuch as the fraction of applicants who were accessioned rose during these ten years. However, the composition of the applicant pool itself might differ over the course of this period. If the average quality—health or otherwise—of the applicant pool increased faster than the overall pool shrank, the corresponding quality of the pool of accessions would actually rise despite a lower nonaccession rate.

Unfortunately, measuring the average health of an accession pool is intrinsically difficult. As found in prior research and briefly discussed in the "Methodology" section above, some potential applicants conceal health conditions.[10] Although we observed failure codes and waivers among all accessions, this information is not consistently col-

---

return the soldier to the point at which that soldier meets medical retention standards. This is called the medical retention determination point. If the soldier does not meet medical retention standards, the soldier is referred for disability evaluation (U.S. Army Medical Command, 2013). The Navy refers a sailor for disability evaluation if "a wound, illness or injury results in a permanent condition or has long-lasting effects" (Navy Wounded Warrior–Safe Harbor, undated). The Air Force Deployment Availability Working Group conducts reviews of service members who have duty-limiting conditions for a cumulative period of 365 days or if a condition is considered unfitting for continued military service. One possible outcome of that review is referral for disability evaluation (U.S. Air Force Surgeon General, 2014).

[10] See Clark, Li, et al., 2000, for calculations with regard to asthma. Similarly, AMSARA concluded that "the current accession screening process fails to identify many disqualifying conditions" because "approximately 2% of all accessions receive an EPTS discharge" while "accessions with most waivers generally do not attrite at a higher rate than those who did not require a waiver" (AMSARA, 2015).

Figure 3.1
Total Number of Applications Annually, by Service, Fiscal Years 2002 Through 2011

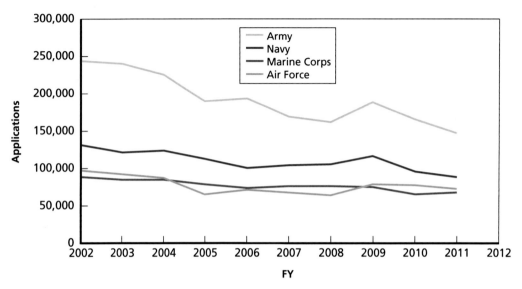

SOURCE: USMEPCOM data.

Figure 3.2
Total Number of Accessions Annually, by Service, Fiscal Years 2002 Through 2011

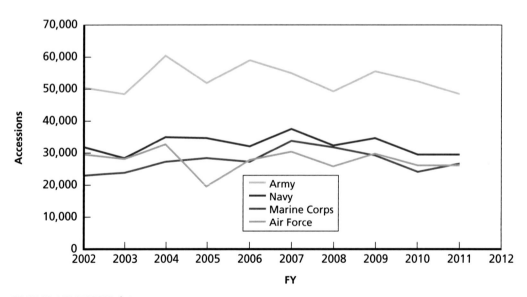

SOURCE: USMEPCOM data.

lected among those who are not accessioned, making it difficult to judge any health condition–specific acceptance rates because we could not fully measure the denominator of such a fraction.

Nevertheless, to provide insight as to whether there is observable temporal variation in the health of new accessions, we examined the fraction of accessions each year who required nonheight, nonweight health waivers. Figure 3.3 indicates a strong variation in this fraction across services and over time. In the Army, for example, this rate rose strongly in 2007 and 2008, before slightly falling. Appendix D contains similar rates of PULHES scores greater than 1 and condition-specific failure codes.[11] The results show substantial temporal and cross-service variation, some of which can be readily explained by events, such as the 2007 Iraq War surge, whereas others are more gradual or do not show substantial variation over time.

Regardless, as discussed above, these measures are a function not just of the health of the applicants but also of the full range of policies that lead to a given health condition resulting in a waiver request; de facto medical standard screening differs because of more than just DoD accession medical standards. Our analysis focused on this specific policy lever.

Figure 3.3
Percentage of Accessions with Nonheight, Nonweight Health Waivers, by Service, Fiscal Years 2002 Through 2011

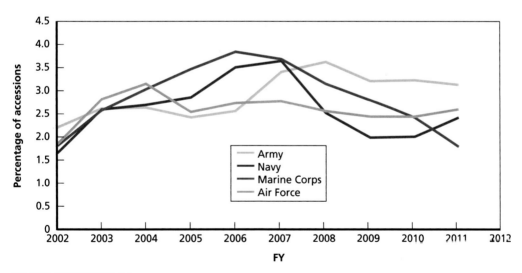

SOURCE: USMEPCOM data.
NOTE: Health waivers exclude nondisease medical waivers (i.e., health and weight disqualifications).

---

[11] A score of 1 indicates a high level of medical fitness, 2 means that the applicant possesses some medical condition that could result in some activity limitations, 3 indicates the presence of one or more medical conditions that could cause significant limitations, and a score of 4 means that the applicant has a medical condition that could be so severe that performance of military duty would have to be drastically limited.

Rates of Medical Discharge

We next turned to these disability outcomes experienced by service members who were accessioned during the FY 2002–2011 period under study. Because we matched the USMEPCOM records of these service members to corresponding DES and IDES disability records (i.e., VTA post-2011, PDCAPS, JDET, and MilPDS), we were able to measure rates of medical discharge both overall and by the presence of specific VASRD codes at various length-of-service horizons.

Figures 3.4 and 3.5 show the fraction of each accession cohort who were medically discharged within the first four and eight YOS, respectively.[12] The Army's rate of medical retirement for this period was two to three times those of the other services. The Marine Corps had the second-highest rate, but it was much closer to those of the Air Force and the Navy. All three services appear to have shown an increase in the rate of medical retirement during this period, although it was most pronounced for the Army.

One concern with a four-year measure, however, is that the disability evaluation process can take a substantial amount of time, and administrative lags can lead to undercounts of disabling conditions that manifested during the first four YOS.

Figure 3.4
Service Members with Medical Retirement in the First Four Years of Service, by Service and Accession Fiscal Year

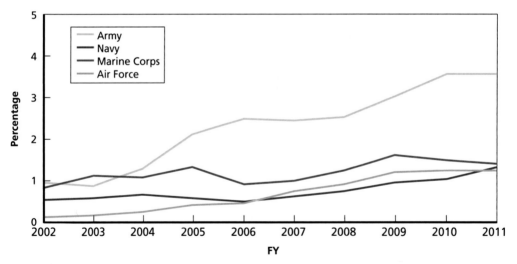

SOURCES: USMEPCOM and disability (VTA, PDCAPS, JDETS, and MilPDS) data.
NOTE: The reported outcome is the percentage of each accession cohort who were medically retired (an overall DoD disability rating of 30 percent or higher) anytime during their first four YOS. People who were accessioned in FY 2011 were the most-recent service members we could follow for four years.

---

[12] Our multivariate analyses looked over five and eight years, but these descriptive figures looked over four and eight.

Figure 3.5
Service Members with Medical Discharge in First Eight Years of Service, by Service and Accession Fiscal Year

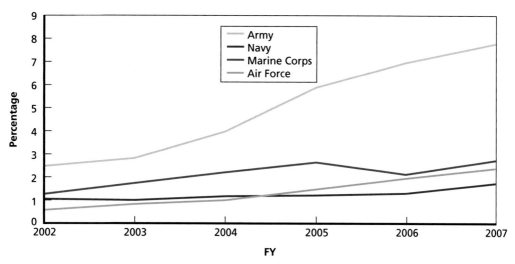

SOURCES: USMEPCOM and disability (VTA, PDCAPS, JDETS, and MilPDS) data.
NOTE: The reported outcome is the percentage of each accession cohort who were medically retired (an overall DoD disability rating of 30 percent or higher) anytime during their first eight YOS. People who were accessioned in FY 2007 were the most-recent service members we could follow for eight years.

The current DoD guidance is that 80 percent of active-duty cases be resolved within 265 days (from referral to discharge; receipt of VA benefits adds another 30 days).[13] In the years of our analysis, the average length of DES often exceeded that (at times, by closer to 400 days per case) (U.S. Government Accountability Office, 2012). To illustrate this concern, Figure 3.5 shows the fraction of medical discharges in the first eight YOS. The trade-off, however, is that we can observe such discharges for only those members who were accessioned early in the period analyzed; those who were accessioned later could not be observed for eight years. The trends across services show an overall increase over time in the percentage of service members accessioned each year who were medically discharged. Companion data showing the rates of medical discharge (regardless of disability rating) by year of accession, as well as medical separations (disability rating less than 30 percent), are in Appendix B.

How much of these differences over time can be accounted for by differences in health at accession? Clearly, there are many reasons medical discharges will vary over time even if service members had exactly the same health at accession: Changes in deployment experiences, retention policies, the DES process itself, and available retraining and rehabilitation options are but a few of these differences. As described

---

[13] For the period we studied, 265 days was per the guidance. Now, under current guidance, this would be 220 days.

previously, our analysis attempted to control for as many of these differences as possible. In addition, we narrowed our analysis to include service members being accessioned as closely in time as possible to one another, yet facing distinct accession medical standards.

Table 3.1 shows the percentage of medical retirements with the most-frequent conditions in the first eight years of service, for service members being accessioned between FYs 2002 and 2007. To step the reader through our analysis, we use knee-related conditions as an example. As Table 3.1 shows, knee-related conditions accounted for between 2 and 3 percent of medical retirements, providing sufficient statistical power to detect how accession medical standard changes affected these outcomes. Although approximately one-quarter of these medical retirements had psychiatric VASRDs, many of which were PTSD, we did not directly include these conditions in our analysis; retention standards and medical practices surrounding PTSD and other psychiatric conditions in general changed substantially during the period under consideration in ways that are difficult to control for and would directly affect medical discharges.

As discussed in Chapter Two, we estimated changes to accession medical standards implemented in three separate years: 2004, 2005, and 2010. To examine the impact that these changes in accession medical standards had on the corresponding

Table 3.1
Percentage of Medical Retirements with the Most-Frequent Conditions in the First Eight Years of Service, for Service Members Being Accessioned Between Fiscal Years 2002 and 2007

Condition	Army (27,469 Retirements Total)	Marine Corps (5,845 Retirements Total)	Navy (3,983 Retirements Total)	Air Force (5,191 Retirements Total)
Any MS	54.7	33.0	25.7	41.3
Lower MS	14.0	11.1	7.9	11.9
Knee	2.4	2.3	1.6	2.7
Any psychiatric	50.3	45.4	38.5	40.7
PTSD	34.6	32.8	13.1	17.5
Asthma	5.9	2.3	1.8	11.0
Colitis	1.3	2.2	6.0	3.6
Migraine	6.3	4.3	3.7	8.1
Epilepsy	1.4	3.1	5.1	2.5
TBI	8.9	8.1	2.4	3.0
None of the above	10.7	18.3	22.8	13.7

NOTE: Because each condition can have more than one VASRD code, percentages can sum to more than 100. MS = musculoskeletal.

conditions, we defined three separate analytic samples with service members undergoing their MEPS medical exams before and after the dates that the DoDI was reissued:

- April 2, 2004: service members whose medical exams occurred between FYs 2002 and 2005, excluding those whose exams occurred within 30 days of the change
- January 18, 2005: service members whose medical exams occurred between FYs 2003 and 2006, excluding those whose exams occurred within 30 days of the change
- April 28, 2010: service members whose medical exams occurred between FYs 2008 and 2011, excluding those whose exams occurred within 30 days of the change.

We arrived at these time periods after considering the trade-off between comparability (i.e., a wider range leads to comparisons across service members with differences that are increasingly unaccounted for by our observable characteristics) and statistical power (i.e., focusing on a narrow bandwidth directly around the policy change limits the number of observations). However, we conducted sensitivity analyses to ensure that, as we narrowed this bandwidth, none of the statistically significant estimates we reported qualitatively changed but merely lost statistical precision.[14] As mentioned previously, we excluded those who were accessioned within one month on either side of the accession medical standard change under consideration to account for anticipation or lags in implementation; including these service members would not have qualitatively changed our findings but added statistical noise to our estimates.

As discussed above, we tested several accession medical standard changes across the three DoDI issuances. There are many more policy changes than the ones we test, because we were limited by two criteria: (1) the condition that was tightened or loosened when the policy changed had to directly correlate to VASRDs, and 2) we needed to have observed a sufficient number of medical discharges with the corresponding VASRDs to allow the statistical identification of an effect. The first point speaks to the internal validity of our study, or whether whatever effect we estimated could be attributed to the policy change we were analyzing. For the second criterion, although MS VASRDs were common among medical discharges across all services, providing sufficient observations to precisely estimate the effects of a change in accession standard, for most other conditions, there are too few observations to provide accurate estimates. That is, the inherent variation in these disabling conditions due to a range of factors we cannot directly observe ("the noise") was stronger than our source of policy variation ("the signal"), which prevented us from inferring direct relationships between accession medical standards and disability outcomes with the data available.

---

[14] The results of our sensitivity analyses are available from the authors upon request.

Limitations of the Analysis

It is worth acknowledging four main limitations in this analytic approach due to the data and policy environment. First, as to the policy-related limitation, the actual adoption of new medical standards by MEPS staff during applicant screening could precede DoDI issuances (if the changes in the issuance were widely discussed beforehand) or lag them (because of diffusion in knowledge and practice in implementing them). Also, USMEPCOM officially implements DoDI policies at a lag, although discussions with USMEPCOM staff have indicated that, upon an issuance, some physicians begin immediately changing their waiver referral processes, while others wait for official implementation or supplemental guidance. In the analysis reported here, we used the date of the DoDI issuances as the tested policy change date; in additional analyses using USMEPCOM supplemental guidance issuances, we found substantially smaller and fewer significant results, but no contradictory results.[15] These findings indicate that, although these supplemental guidance issuances did lead to changes in screening similar to those found with the DoDI issuances, the bulk of the policy implementation appears to occur at the time the DoDI is issued.

The other limitations are related to the available data and limit the scope of the questions this analysis could answer. First, and most importantly, although we observed a range of VASRDs for those service members who were medically discharged, we did not observe the condition or conditions that brought about MEB referral to begin with. Such observation would allow us to focus on "pivotal" conditions, or those conditions that are considered to bring the service member to the medical retention determination point. With this referral data information, we could focus our analysis on which medical standard changes lead service members to no longer meet retention standards, as well as directly test how changes in retention standards affect medical discharges. However, with the current records, these analyses were not feasible.

Second, for the legacy DES (i.e., PDCAPS, JDET, and MilPDS), overall DoD service-connected disability ratings are available, but condition-specific ratings are not available. Hence, subanalyses by severity of medical discharge *of the specific VASRD* were not possible for the vast majority of accession medical standard changes. Third, relatedly, and unfortunately, a large fraction of VTA records for Army service members were missing condition-specific data. That is, VASRDs are unavailable for approximately half of these soldiers post-2012, after new cases were no longer entered into the Army's disability system, PDCAPS. We found no consistent patterns by VASRD

---

[15] In these analyses, to test the additive impact of the supplemental guidance over the prior DoDI reissuance, we also excluded service members who had their MEPS physicals within 30 days of the supplemental guidance. Our findings indicate that there are additional impacts of these supplemental guidance issuances, although they are substantially smaller and less likely to be statistically significant, suggesting that the majority of the effect of a change to a DoD accession medical standard occurs with the original DoDI reissuance.

in the missing status of these data.[16] The analyses presented below assumed that these missing VASRDs were unrelated to the policy change in question—in effect, biasing any estimate toward 0, albeit slightly, given the narrow focus of each test. We tested numerous alternative assumptions,[17] finding no notable differences in our reported effects.

The Effect That Policy Changes Have on Medical Discharges

We now turn to our findings of the relationship between the changes to accession medical standards identified in Chapter Two and downstream medical discharges. We present the corresponding effects for changes in each of the following:

- abdominal
- asthma
- knee
- hearing
- skin and cellular
- endocrine
- elbow
- orthotics.

To demonstrate our full analytic process in arriving at each of these estimates, we present intermediate results for a particular change—the January 2005 DoDI change on knee flexibility—and we illustrate our approach using enlisted Army disability outcomes. Recall that the 2005 policy change tightened the knee-flexibility standard. In 2005, recruits were required to be able to flex each knee 110 degrees, rather than 90 degrees as specified in the 2004 DoDI. In addition, language was added around medial and lateral collateral ligament injuries, medial and lateral meniscal injuries, and internal derangement of the knee, all of which we interpreted as tighter standards.

---

[16] We examined the VASRD mix of medical discharges leading up to and following the transition to VTA, and we found no sharp changes in the fraction of discharges attributed to specific VASRDs or group of VASRDs, suggesting that the missing VASRDs occurred relatively evenly across the range of health conditions and were not concentrated in one specific body system or diagnosis that would lead to spurious conclusions given our research design.

[17] We used three imputation strategies: assuming that no missing VASRDs was the medical discharge outcome of interest (missing $VASRDDis$ = 0), that all missing were the outcome of interest (missing $VASRDDis$ = 1), and randomly assigning to match the mean frequency of the specific VASRD outcome. There were no substantial differences in outcomes, and the results reported correspond to the first assumption—missing VASRDs were coded as not being the outcome of interest. The results of the sensitivity analyses are available upon request.

We fitted the equation described above for knee-related VASRD codes.[18] Figure 3.6 shows the estimated cumulative rates of medical discharge with combined DoD ratings of at least 30 percent, by time in service, for service members who were accessioned before and after the knee policy change, after controlling for all of the variables described earlier in this chapter. As discussed previously, for the 2005 accession medical standard revision, service members who were accessioned before the policy change are those whose most-recent physical exams prior to accession occurred between FY 2003 and 30 days prior to the issuance of the DoDI in April 2005. The post–policy change group included service members whose most-recent physical exams occurred beginning one month after the April 2005 tightening in the accession knee standard, through FY 2006. The "Pre–2005 change" line corresponds to the actual cumulative rates of knee-related medical discharge for those cohorts, whereas we calculated the "Post–2005 change" line from the estimated δs and βs in the regression equation, representing the post–policy change cumulative knee-related medical discharges.

Figure 3.6
Estimated Percentage of Knee-Related Medical Discharges with Combined Ratings of at Least 30 Percent, Pre– and Post–2005 Department of Defense Knee Flexibility Change, Enlisted Army

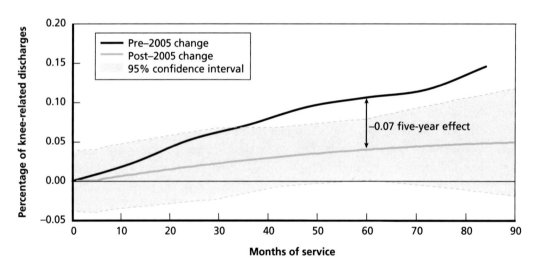

NOTE: The figure includes Army enlisted personnel who were accessioned between FYs 2003 and 2006. It controls for all available covariates. We created the pre–2005 change line using raw data and include it for ease of graphical visualization. Therefore, there is no confidence interval for that cohort. We calculated the post–2005 change line from the estimated δs and βs in the regression equation, representing the post–policy change cumulative knee-related medical discharges.

---

[18] The VASRDs we use for this policy change include: 5256 (knee, ankyloses), 5257 (knee, other impairment), 5258 (cartilage, semilunar, dislocated), 5313 (group XIII function: extension of hip and flexion of knee), and 5314 (group XIV function: extension of knee).

The figure also shows the 95-percent confidence interval for the estimated post–policy change group.

As shown in the figure, the cumulative likelihood of being medically retired with a knee disability fell after the 2005 policy change. This effect appears to have been immediate and persistent, first statistically significantly different from the baseline rate after three years and 0.07 percentage points lower after five years.[19]

Although 0.07 percentage points is not large in absolute magnitude, it represents a 52-percent reduction in the number of knee-related medical discharges (more than half the number of such discharges, given that 0.137 percent of service members who were accessioned before the 2005 policy change had knee-related medical discharges in their first five YOS). For every 10,000 soldiers to be accessioned after the 2005 DoDI knee-flexibility change, the tightening of the knee accession medical standard is associated with a reduction in knee-related medical discharges of seven active-component enlisted soldiers.[20]

A reduction of more than 50 percent in medical discharges is substantial. The analysis covered the years when large numbers of service members were deploying from all services in support of Operation Iraqi Freedom and Operation Enduring Freedom. MS injuries are common during deployments, perhaps especially so for knees and other joints as a result of carrying rucksacks and being on physically demanding missions. It is possible that, to support the deployment tempo, the services were diligent about diagnosing and treating medical conditions that affected readiness. If that happened, the effect that we are attributing to a change in medical standards would also be picking up the increased attention to readiness.

We conducted this same analysis for the other accession medical standard changes discussed in Chapter Two across all four services and report the change in five-year medical discharge rates corresponding to the downstream VASRD disability outcome and combined DoD ratings of at least 30 percent. Earlier, we discussed the reasons for choosing this specification as our baseline and mentioned that two-thirds of all medical discharges were retirements. That represents a DoD average between FYs 2012 and 2016. Because we present our findings by service, it is worth noting that there was some variation by service in the percentage of discharges that were retirements: Approximately 70 and 65 percent of Air Force and Army discharges were retirements, respectively. There was more year-to-year variation for the Marine Corps (45 to 60 percent) and Navy (60 to 70 percent). These results, corresponding to the βs in our regres-

---

[19] This –0.07-percentage-point difference corresponds to the βs evaluated at 60 months of service from our estimated regression equation for knee-related medical discharges with combined ratings of at least 30 percent. For the sake of brevity, we report these differences evaluated at different service horizons for the other changes we estimated.

[20] We calculated this result by multiplying the estimated post–DoDI change knee-related medical discharge rate of –0.000713 percentage points by 10,000 (technically, 7.13 soldiers, which rounds to seven).

sion specification, are shown in Figure 3.7. Appendix E contains results for other definitions of the dependent variable:

- eight-year estimates for overall DoD disability ratings of 30 percent or higher
- five-year estimates for any overall DoD disability rating
- eight-year estimates for any overall DoD disability rating
- five-year estimates for overall DoD disability ratings of less than 30 percent
- eight-year estimates for overall DoD disability ratings of less than 30 percent.

The 2005 tightening of the knee standard also affected other services by reducing their postchange knee medical discharges, although with a lower marginal effect
(and, for the Air Force, not a statistically significant effect). Among the other accession
medical standard changes, some are never statistically associated with a change in disability outcomes—namely, the 2004 loosening of the asthma standard, the loosening
of the 2010 skin and cellular policy change, and the loosening of the 2010 orthotics
standard. These are the only three standards we tested that loosened requirements,
which suggests that loosening these standards did not overall worsen the long-term
health of the affected service members, at least as measured by disability outcomes
(with VASRDs corresponding to the policy changes) during the first five YOS. However, all but one (hearing, 2005) standard that was tightened had a measurable effect
on at least one service.

Abdominal medical standard changes consistently had significant effects, with
the 2004 tightening of these standards substantially reducing medical discharges in
the Marine Corps by 0.09 percentage points and by 0.03 percentage points in the
Navy. The 2005 abdominal standard change caused a reduction of 0.03 percentage
points across the Marine Corps, Navy, and Air Force. However, this standard change
did not have a significant effect on the Army. The 2005 endocrine tightening led to
a statistically and policy-significant reduction in related disability outcomes for the
Marine Corps.

The tightening of the skin and cellular medical standards in 2005, which required
applicants with psoriasis to receive waivers, also led to a statistically significant reduction in the number of medical discharges. This restriction had the largest effect in the
Army, reducing skin-related medical discharges by 0.15 percentage points, and reducing them by 0.06 percentage points in the Marine Corps and 0.03 percentage points
in the Navy.

Finally, the 2010 tightening in the elbow range-of-motion standard led to a reduction in related medical discharges of at least 0.06 percentage points across all services
except the Navy, which experienced a 0.03-percentage-point reduction.

To convert these estimates into the number of service members affected, all
effects reported in Figure 3.7 can be multiplied by the size of the accession cohorts
in the years following the policy change. To standardize this interpretation, each of

Figure 3.7
Effect That Accession Medical Standard Changes Have on the Five-Year Medical Discharge Rate with at Least 30-Percent Rating

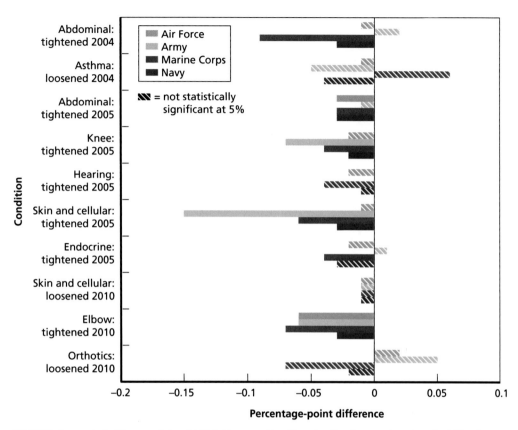

SOURCE: An analytic file containing DMDC, Veterans Tracking Application, and service disability data.
NOTE: The year for each condition indicates the year the governing instruction was published. The bars represent the percentage-point difference in the number of five-year disability retirements for service members who were accessioned after the policy change and those who were accessioned before the change. The five-year disability retirement rate is the percentage of service members who were medical-ly retired by the end of the fifth YOS. To interpret these results, consider a group of 10,000 active-component enlisted service members who were accessioned after the policy change. The effect of the policy change is the effect shown, multiplied by 10,000. For example, the five-year estimate of knee-related disability retirements for the Army is –0.0713 percentage points, which means that the marginal impact in non–percentage point terms is –0.000713, so the estimate implies that there are 0.000713 × 10,000 = 7 (rounded down from 7.13) fewer active-component enlisted soldiers who were medically retired with knee-related discharges after the knee standard was tightened in 2005.

the results in Figure 3.7 can be multiplied by 10,000, which represents the following: For every 10,000 active-component enlisted service members who were accessioned after the policy change, that many more or fewer would be medically discharged with VASRDs corresponding to the policy. Table 3.2 summarizes these results for a hypothetical group of 10,000 service members who were accessioned after each of the policy changes examined were issued. To put these results into context, Table 3.2 also

Table 3.2
Effect That Accession Medical Standard Changes Have on the Number of Five-Year Medical Discharges with at Least 30-Percent Ratings, per 10,000 Service Members

Cohort	Army	Marine Corps	Navy	Air Force
2004				
Active-component enlisted accessions	72,710	30,156	39,416	33,690
Abdominal (tightened)	2	–9**	–3**	–1
Asthma (loosened)	–5	6	–4	–1
2005				
Active-component enlisted accessions	63,324	32,015	37,729	19,092
Knee (tightened)	–7***	–4***	–2**	–2
Abdominal (tightened)	–1	–3***	–3***	–3***
Hearing (tightened)	0	–4	–1	–2
Skin and cellular (tightened)	–15***	–6***	–3***	–1
Endocrine (tightened)	1	–4***	–3	–2
2010				
Active-component enlisted accessions	70,081	28,018	34,048	28,363
Elbow (tightened)	–6**	–7**	–3***	–6**
Skin and cellular (loosened)	–1	–1	–1	–1
Orthotics (loosened)	5	–7	–2	2

SOURCES: OUSD(P&R), 2004, Table B.1; OUSD(P&R), 2005a, Table B-1; OUSD(P&R), 2010a, Table B.1.

NOTE: For every 10,000 service members who were accessioned after a policy change, we show the number we estimate will be medically discharged within five years with a disability related to the policy change more or fewer than those who were accessioned before the policy change. The five-year disability retirement rate is the percentage of service members who were medically retired by the end of the fifth YOS. ** = statistically significant at 5%; *** = statistically significant at 1%.

includes the size of each service's active-component enlisted accession cohort for each of the three policy-change years. Recall from above that these policy changes went into effect in the middle of these FYs, so some accessions in those years joined before the policy change. Therefore, these accession cohort numbers serve the purpose of providing context, but it would be straightforward to multiply the 10,000–service member estimate by the size of a future accession cohort.

Conclusions

We can draw some conclusions from these findings. First, our analytic approach had sufficient statistical power to measure how certain changes in accession medical standards affected downstream, related medical discharges, provided that there were sufficient number of medical discharges of the corresponding type. Second, we did find that accession medical standards have an effect on the likelihood of medical discharge, even after controlling for a rich set of individual characteristics and service experiences. This effect varies substantially across services, and, as the knee example (and other results in Appendix E) showed, it is not limited to discharges occurring at the beginning of terms of service, with differences in these specific medical discharge outcomes often increasing through the first eight YOS. However, as a reminder, discharges that occur in the eighth YOS represent injuries or illnesses that were detected, for the most part, during the first six YOS (followed by up to one year of treatment and an approximately year-long disability evaluation). And, as we show in Chapter Four, the third through fifth YOS are when the largest percentage of discharges occurred during the period covered by this analysis.

Third, the major loosenings under study did not appear to increase subsequent medical discharges, while all but one of the tightenings (hearing, 2005) led to a statistically significant reduction in downstream disability retirement outcomes (the tightening of the hearing standard was correlated with a lower probability of medical discharges, unconditional on rating). In other words, those allowed to join after a loosening in accession medical standards were not more likely to be medically discharged with corresponding disabilities, while those who were held to a higher medical standard after a policy tightening were less likely to be discharged with a corresponding disability. If a central concern over whether to loosen an accession medical standard is how subsequent medical discharges might increase, our findings indicate that, for the three loosenings we studied, there was no indication of such an increase. Additionally, if one aim of tightening medical standards is to decrease medical discharges, we found that nearly all of the tightenings we studied often led to such decreases.

However, there is variation in the effect according to the type of the accession medical standard change, with changes to medical standards for some body systems having consistent effects for certain services, while others were specific to one condition:

- The three internal body system changes—namely, the 2004 and 2005 abdominal changes and the 2005 endocrine change—had statistically significant effects on disability outcomes but varied widely by branch of service.
- The 2005 change to skin and cellular, pertaining to psoriasis, had the largest effects found.

- The two motion or flexibility standard changes we tested, the 2005 knee and 2010 elbow changes, had consistently large effects identified, especially for soldiers and marines.
- The tightening of the 2005 hearing standard resulted in marginally significant effects for some services (Marine Corps and Navy) when the outcome of interest was all disability discharges (retirements and separations), as shown in Appendix E.
- The Marine Corps was the service most consistently affected by tightening accession medical standards, with only one tightening not producing a statistically significant negative effect.
- The estimated effects on medical separations (i.e., medical discharges with combined ratings of less than 30 percent; shown in Appendix E) are small and rarely statistically significant, indicating that the primary impact of changes in accession medical standards is on discharges with ratings of at least 30 percent.

Several individual characteristics were associated with medical discharge. Service members who had ever deployed and who were deployed three years ago were more likely to be medically discharged. On the other hand, the more deployments a service member has, the less likely that member is to be medically discharged. This is a selection effect: Those service members whose health is good (and who are therefore not likely to be referred for disability evaluation) are the ones who are able to participate in multiple deployments. We also found that a higher BMI was generally associated with an increased probability of being medically discharged across the policy changes we tested. Other control variables, such as occupation and pay grade, are statistically significant in most of our regressions, but patterns vary.

A question that follows naturally from an analysis like this is whether the specific policy effects on disability outcomes from past changes in accession medical standards can be extrapolated to the future, or whether the model can be used to predict how future changes in standards would affect disability outcomes. The short answer to both of those questions is "no." The analytic file that we used to conduct the analyses in this report included service members who were accessioned between FYs 2002 and 2011. Each had a specific set of individual characteristics, including health status, that contributed to the probability of being medical discharged through the DES. Members who are accessioned in the future will almost certainly look different from those accessioned in the past, and policy changes in the same body system could lead to different effects. So even if a policy change could be replicated in the future, downstream disability outcomes would almost certainly be different. Further, to use the model that we developed—which we built at the person-year level—to predict future medical discharges, we would have to populate all of the variables for which we controlled, for every service member in every YOS. This includes specific events, such as the number of cumulative deployments and the service member's pay grade at a point in time. Because doing this is not possible, we cannot reliably estimate future disability outcomes using this framework.

However, the model estimates that resulted from our analysis are rich in information about how individual and service characteristics are correlated with medical discharges and provide estimates of effects over long observation periods—findings that are useful for thinking about future outcomes. Although using data on accessions that occurred from 2002 to 2011 limits direct applicability to current service members, one notable conclusion from our analysis is that, by following these service members for up to eight YOS, changing medical standards continues to affect medical discharges throughout this time period.

Finally, this chapter (along with Appendix D) presents data on the percentage of service members accessioned in a given year who received nonheight, nonweight health waivers, PULHES scores greater than 1, and medical failure codes. Future research delving more deeply into the waiver referral and approval processes could lead to additional policies to limit costly medical discharges with etiologies tracing to observable conditions at accession. However, such questions were beyond the scope of this analysis, although we nevertheless found that official accession medical standards themselves play an important role in the evolution of disability rates and types in each of the services.

In the next chapter, we construct and execute a systematic method for translating the size and trajectory of the effects presented in this chapter into corresponding monetary costs.

CHAPTER FOUR

Cost Analysis

In Chapter Three, we showed that several changes to accession medical standards between 2004 and 2010 were correlated with corresponding changes in disability outcomes. In other words, service members who were accessioned after standards were tightened were medically retired at a lower rate than those who were accessioned prior to the policy change. The output of our analysis in Chapter Three was the change in the probability of being medically discharged after a change in accession medical standards. For all results that were statistically significant (which included only tightened standards), in this chapter, we provide estimates of what those changes in probabilities mean in terms of the cost associated with the changes in accession medical standards. Put another way, if accession medical standards are tightened and fewer service members who are accessioned under the new policy are medically discharged, how much money does DoD save?

To estimate the potential cost of changes in accession medical standards, we developed a simple model of postservice costs and compared model estimates under a baseline scenario with estimates under a scenario in which medical discharge is less likely (to be consistent with the policy tightening results from Chapter Three). The model is straightforward: A service member can leave (exit) active service in a fixed number of ways, and each exit method has an associated probability and an associated cost. Both the probability and the cost vary by YOS. We estimated the probability and postservice cost for each YOS and combined them in a weighted sum as the expected, postservice cost of a recruit. Then, using the coefficient estimates from our policy evaluation in Chapter Three, we adjusted the probabilities of each exit method to reflect the change in the probability of medical discharge.[1] We recalculated the expected cost; the difference between the baseline estimate and the policy-changed estimate is our estimate of the cost (or savings) associated with changing accession medical standards.

---

[1] In Chapter Three, we presented estimates for medical retirement, which represents two-thirds of all medical discharges and accounts for most of the policy effect, as evidenced by the small, usually not statistically significant effects for separations. We used the changes in the probability of medical retirement in the cost model and included the cost of medical separations in the cost estimates.

Although we refer throughout to the *cost model*, it is more accurate to think of our analysis as a comparative cost exercise or an accounting exercise. The term *model* can imply that we evaluated the specific policy and examined affected accession cohorts to estimate the budgetary change in costs. Instead, we used the relative magnitudes of exit costs to demonstrate a source of potential cost changes associated with a policy that affects exit probabilities.

We now describe our model, the data used to populate the probabilities and costs for each type of exit, and our results.

Scope of the Model

Our analysis in Chapter Three estimated the relationship between changes in accession medical standards and exiting military service with a medical disability. Hence, we built our cost model to measure the changes in cost *after* exit. Specifically, we estimated the postservice cost to DoD resulting from the accession medical policy changes as reflected in the change of probability of medical discharge. These costs include DoD-provided cash payments to retirees and DoD-provided health care coverage; anyone with a medical or career retirement is eligible for both of these for the retiree's lifetime. We also estimated the one-time costs associated with medical separation. It is important to note that we were interested in DoD costs, not combined costs to the government; thus, the costs we estimated exclude payments made or services provided by VA, the U.S. Social Security Administration, or the U.S. Treasury. Put another way, our cost model answers the following question: If DoD changes accession medical standards, do those changes affect DoD's long-term, postservice financial obligations?

Although our model includes the costs of health care and cash compensation, three key costs that we did not include in our model would likely change the bottom-line DoD cost. First, our model does not include the costs of replacing or retaining service members. If service members are more likely to be medically discharged, the number of new recruits needed to replace them, or the number of active service members who would need to be retained in their absence, would need to increase. Recruiting and retention are associated with steep costs, from advertising and recruiters to bonuses. Although the accession medical policies described in Chapter Three are associated with relatively small effects—ranging from a decrease of two to 15 service members being medically retired per 10,000 new accessions—previous studies have found that even the marginal cost of recruiting alone could be up to $33,000 per recruit (Asch, Heaton, et al., 2010).

In addition, we did not incorporate the costs of the Survivor Benefit Plan (SBP), an insurance policy into which retirees can elect to pay that provides a covered survivor a cash annuity in the event of the sponsor's death. The lifetime cost of medical retirement in our model includes cash benefits paid to the retiree and the retiree's health care, but not the obligations to the retiree's family after the retiree's death. Again, these could be significant exclusions; DoD pays nearly half of the SBP premium. A recent study estimated that the present discounted value of cumulative benefits over 30 years for childless survivors is $0.8 million; for survivors with two children, it is $1.09 million (Hosek, Asch, Mattock, Gutierrez, et al., 2018). However, incorporating this cost would require numerous assumptions about the share of medical retirees who elect SBP coverage and the scope of coverage (spouse, former spouse, child, disabled dependent, or person with natural insurable interest).

Finally, we did not include what we refer to as transaction, or maintenance, costs. Service members referred for disability evaluation incur administrative costs as they are evaluated and processed, and they must be fed, clothed, and cared for in the meantime. We focused instead on postservice costs: We examined exit effects and did not include these transactional costs.

Hence, the cost model that we present in this chapter should be thought of as a *notional* model. It is not a true budgetary formulation but an estimate of hypothetical magnitudes of cost savings in one context (postservice) and for one stakeholder (DoD). Any estimate of cost described in this chapter should not be thought of as a true budgetary savings because neither the Comptroller General of the United States nor Congress can reappropriate the money.

And, we note, our model does not include the unquantifiable cost or benefit of being able to serve in the military or the benefits that DoD and the nation experience from an individual service member's contributions. Our model calculates the cost saving from tighter medical standards in accession medical policy, but there is an intangible cost to the people who are not allowed to serve that we cannot account for.

Model Framework and Assumptions

Our model calculates the expected postservice cost of an individual active-component enlistee. This expected cost is a function of two things: probability of exiting the military through each potential path and the corresponding cost of each exit method. At each YOS, an active-component enlistee has a finite set of possible states in the next YOS. We defined eight states: (being retained as an) active-component enlistee, officer, reservist, death, nonmedical separation, medical separation, career retirement, and medical retirement.[2] There is a probability of reaching each state in each YOS, and each state has a corresponding cost in each YOS. Figure 4.1 illustrates the different possible states for an active-component enlistee.

---

[2] Nonmedical separation is largely voluntary separation at the end of a term but also includes involuntary separation, so these are grouped together as "nonmedical."

Figure 4.1
Model Framework: Exit Probabilities

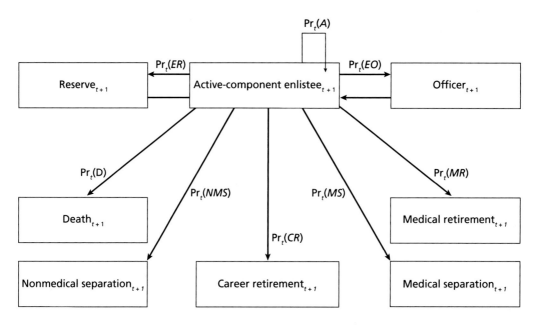

In YOS 0, an enlistee joins the active component. In the subsequent YOS t, there is a probability Pr that the enlistee will exit into one of the seven other possible states, j. Every year has a YOS-specific probability of flowing out to each state that is specific to the number of years an enlistee has served. Every state has a YOS-specific cost. Mathematically, the expected cost (*EC*) postservice that DoD incurs for an active-duty enlistee can be expressed as a sum of the costs associated with each state j in each YOS t, weighted by the probability Pr of reaching that state in that year:

$$EC = \sum_t \sum_j \mathrm{Pr}_t(j) \times cost_t^j.$$

To be expressed as an expected cost, each *cost* in each YOS t is discounted back to its value in YOS 0 or, assuming a discount factor of 5.25 percent[3],

$$cost_t = \frac{\text{cost in YOS}_t}{(1.0525)^t}.$$

We estimated the cost of an accession medical policy based on its effect on the probability of reaching certain states. That is, we assumed that the *cost* of each state in

---

[3]   Later in this chapter, we discuss discounting, but we use the discount rate (5.25 percent) used in *Statistical Report on the Military Retirement System*.

each year would not be affected by the policy but that the *probability* of reaching that state would be affected, which changes the probability of reaching the other states. For example, a change in accession medical policy that decreases the probability of being medically retired, $\text{Pr}_t(MR)$, in the fifth YOS does not change the cost of medical retirement with five YOS. It will, however, result in an increase in the probability of remaining in the active component or in any other state. Because the sum of the probabilities for the eight states must sum to 1, if one probability increases or decreases, one or more of the other states must move in the opposite direction.

We have described the mechanics of our model so far as one person, who, in each YOS, has a probability of exiting into each state. It can be more intuitive, however, to think instead of a group. For simplicity, consider 100 new recruits entering the active component. In each YOS, the number of active-component service members decreases as members exit into other states so that, by the time the last service member completes service, 14 will have retired with at least 20 YOS, four will have medically retired, two will have medically separated, and the rest will have exited at the end of the term or transferred to the reserves. Our baseline model calculates the expected cost to DoD (cash compensation and health care benefits) given the exit states of the initial 100 service members.

Suppose that, under a policy tightening, the probability of being medically discharged decreases, such that, instead of four service members medically retiring and two medically separating, the new numbers are three and one. The decrease in the probability of medical discharge increases the probability of career retirement and voluntary withdrawal. The two service members who did not medically discharge can now retire or separate at the end of the term, for instance. We then recalculated the expected cost to DoD of the 100 service members, with the new distribution of exit states. Regardless of whether there is one service member, 100, or an entire accession cohort, the probability of each exit state and each YOS sums to 1, and the cost is the weighted sum of those probability and the cost of each exit state.

The cost of the policy is thus the difference of the two expected costs, one based on a baseline probability vector and the other based on a probability vector permuted by changes to the likelihood of medical discharge:

$$EC_{policy} = \left(\sum_t \sum_j \text{Pr}_t(j) \times cost_t^j \right) - \left(\sum_t \sum_j \text{Pr}_{t,policy}(j) \times cost_t^j \right).$$

Hence, estimating the model required a baseline probability matrix consisting of eight vectors, one for each state, over 35 possible YOS,[4] as well as a varied probability

---

[4] A service member can serve longer than 35 years. In our probability model, however, the probability of remaining in service longer than 35 years is so low that it rounds down to 0. Hence, the model assumes that service occurs from 0 to 35 years.

matrix that incorporates into each probability vector the accession medical policy's effect and a cost matrix consisting of eight vectors, one for each state, over 35 YOS.

In the next section, we discuss the probabilities and costs that populate the state-by-year vectors. Like the analysis described in Chapter Three, our cost model is restricted to active-component enlisted service members. As we show later, to estimate health care costs, which we calculated based on age and not YOS, we needed to assume an age at the time of enlistment; in our baseline specification, we used age 19. We could measure the model's sensitivity to the starting age and estimate the effect of the policy if the starting age of enlistees varies between 19 and 22.

State Probabilities and Costs

State Probabilities

The model as presented in Figure 4.1 requires the estimation of seven state-by-YOS probability vectors, one for each exit state (career retirement, medical retirement, medical separation, officer, reserve, death, and nonmedical separation) and the remainder, those who remain in the active component, is 1 minus those probabilities.

We obtained the probability vectors from OACT. OACT based these probabilities on the observed, historical trajectories of prior and active service members. OACT used the probabilities in its calculations of DoD's future financial obligations and the solvency of trust funds covering those obligations.

Four of the probabilities enumerated in our model—career retirement, medical retirement, death, and officer—are provided directly by OACT.[5] In addition, OACT combined two states—nonmedical separation and reserve—into a single probability, to which it refers as withdrawal. We did not have a means of dividing the single withdrawal probability into the composite probabilities of nonmedical separation (voluntary or involuntary) and transfers to the reserve. Doing so would entail a significant number of assumptions. Moreover, it was not necessary to divide them because their costs were not calculated, which we discuss in more detail in the next section. The remaining state, retention as an active-component enlistee, is the residual probability when the others have been subtracted and can be calculated simply. Hence, the only probability vector of the seven needed for the model that we do not give is that of medical separation, those who are awarded less than 30-percent disability ratings.

To calculate the percentage of active-component enlistees who medically separate, we used VTA disability data to calculate the relative ratio of medical separa-

---

[5]   The probability vectors published by OACT are conditional vectors; they are the YOS exit probability, conditional on being in that YOS. For the expected per-recruit cost, we converted the conditional probability into unconditional probability. The probability vectors by YOS can be found in OACT, 2016b, Appendix G: death rates (Table G2), retirement rates by disability status (Table G4), withdrawal and reentrant (Table G6), and transfer to officer (Table G8).

tions to medical retirements, or the average ratio of those with disability ratings below 30 percent relative to those at or above 30 percent. We found that, of all medical discharges, approximately two-thirds are retirements and one-third are separations, so there are twice as many retirements as there are separations. With this average ratio, we were able to calculate a probability of medical separation based on OACT's medical retirement vector and subtract those medical separations from the withdrawal probability to create a new, separate probability vector.

Finally, OACT includes a state that we have not yet discussed: a reentrant category, for members transferring from officer, reservist, or extended-leave status into the active-component enlisted force. This is not a state, per se, because it does not have a cost, but we included the probability in our model.

We made an assumption about the interaction of the probability vectors. We assumed that the probability of becoming an officer, transferring to the reserve component, or dying is not affected by changes to accession medical policies. That is, the share of a starting cohort that flows to these states in each year is fixed in reference to the policy changes we examined. We made these assumptions about officer and reserve component transfer mainly because of the scope of our policy effects—we did not estimate the primary effect that changes in medical standards in accession have on the probability of transferring to the reserve component or becoming an officer, nor did we estimate the secondary effect on posttransfer exits. Hence, we did not make any assumptions about either and assumed that the transfer and the costs of exits, once transferred, were the same. We made a similar assumption that the flow of reentrants was not affected by disability policy.

The assumption about the transition to the reserve component might have had an impact on our cost estimates. A 2011 RAND study reported the transition rate from the active component to the selected reserves within two years of leaving the active component. The average rate between 1998 and 2008 ranged from 5 percent in the Marine Corps to 15 percent in the Army (Hosek and Miller, 2011). Service members who leave the active component and join the reserve component might serve long enough to retire. We did not include that probability or the costs associated with this transfer, which means that regular retirement costs were underestimated in our model. In addition, we did not include the possibility that a service member who transferred from the active component to the reserve component can be subsequently medically discharged. The amount by which our model underestimates career retirement likely outweighs the amount by which it underestimates medical retirements, which would result in an overstatement of the cost savings associated with changing medical standards.

Figure 4.2 shows, for each YOS, the rate at which active-component enlisted service members end up in each state. The majority of enlistees will withdraw from the active component and will do so within the first eight YOS, as shown in the top panel. Starting in the 20th YOS (labeled as 19 completed YOS because YOS begins with 0

Figure 4.2
Rates of Exit from Active-Component Enlistees' Accumulated Military Service, by Type of Exit and Year of Service, Withdrawals and All Others

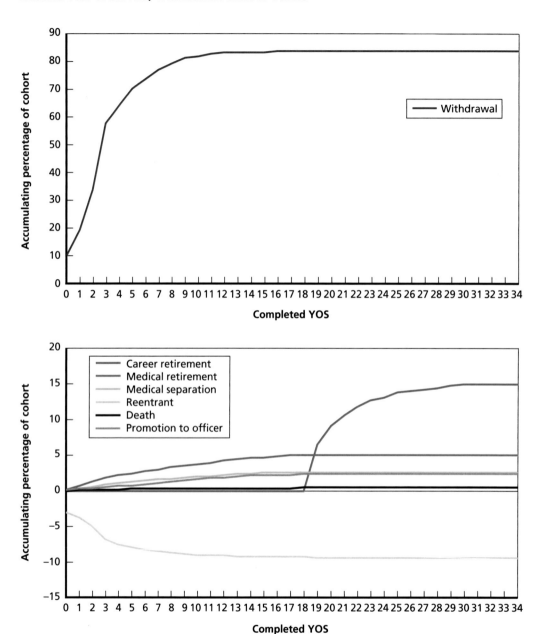

SOURCES: OACT, 2016b, Tables G2, G4, G6, and G8; medical separation values calculated from VTA.
NOTE: The medical separation line is nearly identical to the one for "Promotion to Officer." A small portion of the line is visible in the early YOS but is otherwise masked by the officer line.

in this model), the year in which an enlistee is eligible for career retirement, the probability of retiring increases; again, the majority of career retirees will separate in the first few years following retirement eligibility. By comparison, the percentage of active-component enlistees who die, become an officer, medically separate, or medically retire is very small. We followed OACT and assumed that the final YOS is 35 (OACT does not provide estimates beyond 35 completed YOS).

The value of each line for the final YOS is the final probability of ending at each state. The majority of active-component enlistees (83.7 percent) will withdraw from the active component, 2.4 percent will become officers, 0.5 percent will die, 2.6 percent will medically separate, 5.1 percent will medically retire, and 15.0 percent will reach career retirement. These numbers do not sum to 100 because of the reentrant values (see the line shown in Figure 4.2), which are negative.

The effect of accession medical policies estimated and presented in Chapter Three would be to directly alter the shape of the medical retirement probability curve in the first five YOS by the amounts shown in Figure 3.7 in Chapter Three (and illustrated for the knee example in Figure 3.6 in the same chapter) and, as a result, indirectly alter the remaining probabilities. Given our assumption that the probability of reentrance, promotion to officer, change to reservist, and death are not influenced by changes in accession medical standards, the probabilities that absorb the change in the probability of medical retirement are nonmedical separation, medical separation, career retirement, and the stock state, being retained as an active-component enlistee.

To clarify, in Chapter Three, we reported our estimate of the effect that changes to accession medical standards have on the probability of medically retiring, and the cost model in this chapter directly estimates the cost of the change in medical retirement probability. We calculated the probability of medical separation used in our model as a fixed ratio to medical retirement because OACT did not provide it separately. Hence, if we tested policy effects from the regression coefficients on both, we would be double counting the change in medical separation, first from the ratio to medical retirement and second from the regression coefficient changes. For that reason, and because the postservice cost of medical separation is trivial compared to the postservice cost of medical retirement, as we discuss in the next section, we tested only the policy effect *directly* on medical retirement. We lost some precision in doing so.

Figure 4.3 shows the same rates of exit as Figure 4.2, but only for medical separation, medical retirement, and career retirement. The figure demonstrates the relevance of our analysis—approximately half of medically retiring enlisted service members leave in the first five YOS, the window of our policy analysis. It also demonstrates a shortcoming: that the other half of all discharges occur after those five years, and not enough time has elapsed since the policy changes examined in this study to speak to later-year effects of changes to accession standards.

Figure 4.4 shows the distribution of YOS for medical retirees observed in the two most-recent years of available data in another way. Rather than the rates of discharge

Figure 4.3
Rates of Exit from Active-Component Enlistees' Accumulated Military Service, by Type of Exit and Year of Service, Career Retirement and Medical Discharge

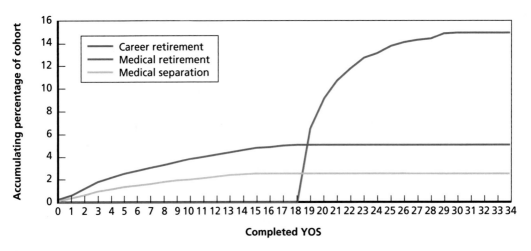

SOURCES: OACT, 2016b, Table G4; medical separation data calculated from VTA.
NOTE: The figure presents the same data as in Figure 4.2 but with different y-axis specifications and fewer series to narrow in on the outcomes associated with cash compensation and health care costs to DoD upon a service member's discharge from active-component enlisted service.

Figure 4.4
Distribution of Completed Years of Service Among Service Members Who Were Medically Retired in Fiscal Year 2013

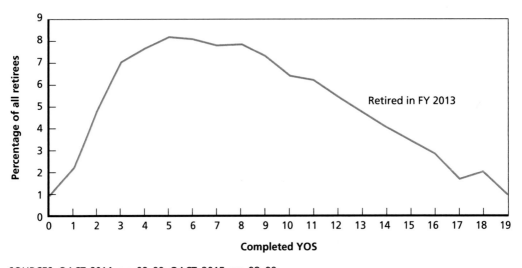

SOURCES: OACT, 2014, pp. 98–99; OACT, 2015, pp. 98–99.
NOTE: This series shows, among the population of active-component enlistees who medically retired in FY 2013, the percentage who had completed that number of YOS at the time of retirement.

by YOS into exit states, it shows the percentage of service members who medically retire in each YOS. For example, of all medical retirees who left the service in FY 2013, 8 percent were in their sixth YOS.

Department of Defense Costs

Like with the probabilities, the model, as illustrated in Figure 4.1, requires the estimation of eight state-by-YOS cost vectors, one for each exit state and the reentrant category. In practice, however, we did not need to estimate each vector. Given the assumption that the probability of reentering, becoming an officer, becoming a reservist, or dying does not change with accession medical standards, those costs did not need to be calculated separately. They were differenced out in the model when we subtracted the expected cost after a policy change from the baseline expected cost.

In addition, like we noted earlier, we calculated only the *postservice* cost to DoD of policies, not the current-period cost or cost to agencies outside of DoD. As a consequence, we assumed that the cost of the stock state—remaining an active-component enlistee—was 0. In reality, this is not accurate. Active-component enlistees must be housed, fed, clothed, and paid. But active-component enlistees also benefit the armed forces with their service, which we also did not attempt to calculate. An alternative way to phrase this assumption is that the postservice cost of the stock state was absorbed via exits from other states only. Note that, if we were calculating effects on replacement or retention from the medical standard policy change, this state *would* have a cost.

Similarly, we assumed nonmedical separation, such as when a service member voluntarily leaves at the end of a term, to have zero postservice costs. Again, this is not the case in practice, in that exiting service members who have successfully completed the term are eligible for an array of benefits, such as education support, business start-up support, and job-search support. However, some or all of these types of benefits are paid and coordinated through organizations and departments other than DoD, and this cost analysis is for DoD costs only. A zero postservice cost for nonmedical separation reflects that DoD has no financial obligations to those former service members.

Hence, only three states require state-by-YOS postservice DoD cost calculation: medical separation, medical retirement, and career retirement. Again, given the assumptions in our model and our focus on postservice *differences* in DoD obligations, the costs in our model were notional estimates, not budgetary equivalents.

We now turn to the cost data that we used in our model.

Medical Separation: Postservice Department of Defense–Provided Severance Pay and Health Benefits

A service member who medically separates with a disability rating of less than 30 percent is eligible for a one-time severance payment and 180 days of continued health care benefits. The amount of the one-time severance payment is calculated using a formula based on base pay at time of exit and the number of years of completed service: 2 × YOS × monthly basic pay. The line in Figure 4.5 shows the FY 2015 monthly basic pay of enlistees, weighted by distribution of ranks in each YOS.[6] Monthly basic pay ranges from approximately $2,000 in the first YOS to nearly $4,000 in the 19th YOS. The bars show the calculated medical separation one-time severance payout. In the initial YOS, the amount is just under $4,000, but, by the 19th year, it is as large as $150,000.

Medically separated service members are also eligible for 180 days of health care coverage. To calculate this cost, we used estimates from OACT's financial statement supplement to the valuation of the Medicare-Eligible Retiree Health Care Fund (MERHCF), which gives average annual health care costs of nonactive service members eligible for DoD health benefits who are not Medicare eligible (i.e., under age 65)

Figure 4.5
Weighted Monthly Basic Pay for Enlistees and Calculated Medical Severance Payout, by Year of Service at the Time of Medical Separation

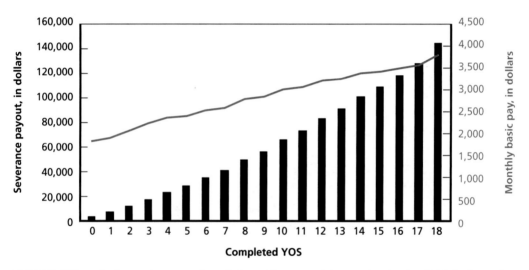

SOURCES: Military basic-pay data come from Defense Finance and Accounting Service, 2015. Basic pay is weighted by rank of service members leaving the active component with permanent disability (OACT, 2016a, p. 127).
NOTE: The line, measured on the right axis, shows monthly base pay weighted by rank. The bars are measured on the left axis and show the one-time severance payment made to those who are medically separated.

---

[6] Monthly basic pay comes from the January 1, 2015, publication from the Defense Finance and Accounting Service (Defense Finance and Accounting Service, 2015), which gives basic-pay tables by pay grade and rank. These basic-pay amounts are then weighted by the number of service members in each rank who leave the active component with disability ratings from *Statistical Report on the Military Retirement System* (OACT, 2016a, p. 127).

by age of sponsor (the former service member).[7] Critically, this estimate includes costs for any family members who also receive coverage. These health care estimates are the same as the ones used for retirees, and we discuss them in more detail in the next section. However, to calculate the cost of a half-year of coverage for a medically separated enlistee, we took the estimate of the health care costs of the assumed age of the medically separated service member and divided it in half because we did not have data on the cost of the 180-day benefit. Estimates range from $2,000 to $4,000 for 180 days of health care. If separatees consume a lot of health care during this time, actual costs could be higher; they might also be lower if the separatee has other coverage. By law, TRICARE is the second payer.

Postservice Department of Defense–Provided Retirement Cash Compensation and Health Benefits

Medical retirement occurs when a service member exits with a disability rating of at least 30 percent, regardless of years served. Career retirement occurs when a service member fulfills at least 20 YOS. A retiree, whether medical or career, receives a monthly cash payout from DoD based on the number of completed YOS or disability rating that lasts until death.[8] A retiree is also eligible for health benefits for themselves and dependents until the retiree's death.[9] To compare the total benefit for which retirees are eligible, we calculated the present discounted cost of both the stream of DoD-provided cash payments and the DoD-provided health care coverage for the retiree's lifetime.[10]

We calculated the present discounted cost of cash payments and health care benefits by multiplying the expected payment at retirement by the length of time for which it is received, adjusted for the real discount rate for that length of time. On the cash side, this is referred to as the lump-sum equivalent. In *Statistical Report on the Military Retirement System*, the lump-sum equivalent is provided for career retirees, using an assumed annual cost-of-living adjustment of 2.75 percent and a discount rate of 5.25 percent. We used the same rates to calculate the medical retirees' lump-sum equivalent and conferred with OACT to verify that our estimates for medical retirees

---

[7]   The supplement is OACT's financial statement published in January 2017 (OACT, 2017) to accompany the report *Valuation of the Medicare-Eligible Retiree Health Care Fund*, published in December 2016 (OACT, 2016b).

[8]   We calculated this as 0.025 × YOS × basic pay. In the case of medical retirees, an alternative formula is disability rating × basic pay, plus any concurrent payments for which the service member might be eligible, such as concurrent retirement disability pay for those eligible for both military retired pay and VA compensation or, for someone with combat-related disability, combat-related special compensation.

[9]   A veteran with a service-connected disability, which includes someone medically retired or separated, is also eligible for health care from VA, but, as mentioned earlier, in this model, we captured only costs incurred by DoD.

[10]   We refer to this as present discounted cost because we used the government discount rate. Another common discounting method is present discounted value, which is the value to the service member and relies on a personal discount rate.

were comparable to the provided estimates for career retirees.[11] On the health care cost side, we used economic assumptions provided in the MERHCF report for FY 2015—a 5.5-percent long-term medical trend growth rate and 5.25-percent discount rate—and calculated the present value of lifetime health care costs for both medical and career retirees.[12] We assumed, per the MERHCF, that medical retiree life expectancy is 76 and career retiree life expectancy is 80. All costs expressed are in 2015 dollars.

Figure 4.6 shows the lump-sum equivalent of lifetime payouts for medical and career retirees. On average, the lump-sum equivalent for career retirees is higher, driven by additional YOS and higher ranks that result in a higher principal benefit amount. A service member who medically retires in the first few YOS receives a lifetime total of nearly $400,000, and one who retires (medically or by YOS) at close to 20 years receives around $700,000 in cash payouts over a lifetime.

Retirees and their dependents are also eligible for health care for their lifetimes. Figure 4.7 displays the annual average costs of a medical retiree and a career retiree, by

Figure 4.6
Lump-Sum Equivalent of Lifetime Department of Defense–Provided Retired Pay, by Years of Service, Fiscal Year 2015

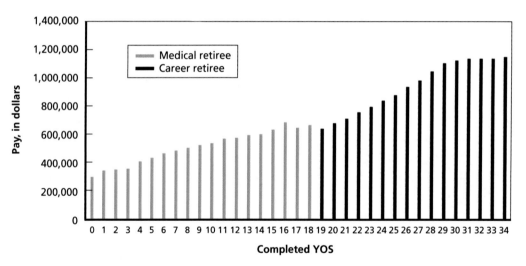

SOURCES: OACT, 2016a, p. 279, weighted by observed rank of retirees, and estimates provided by OACT.
NOTE: Lump-sum payouts assume a 2.75-percent cost-of-living adjustment and 5.25-percent annual discount rate, and the mortality expectation is calculated differently for disabled and nondisabled retirees. Mortality expectations are 76 for medical retirees and 80 for career retirees, which can be found in the FY 2015 MERHCF valuation report (OACT, 2016a).

---

[11] The career retirees' lump-sum equivalents can be found at OACT, 2016a, p. 279, and the assumptions of growth at OACT, 2016a, p. 282. For the medical retirees, OACT provided us with a memo, "Lump Sum Equivalent Value of Retired Pay for Disability Retirees," which is available upon request.

[12] These rates are also comparable to the real growth rates of military health costs used in Congressional Budget Office, 2014.

Figure 4.7
Average Annual Health Care Costs to the Department of Defense for Medical and Career Retirees, by Age, Fiscal Year 2015

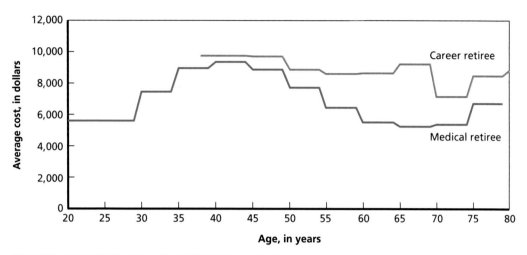

SOURCES: OACT, 2016b, Table E3; OACT, 2017, pp. 16–30.
NOTE: This figure shows the average costs per retiree for one year of health care, including dependent coverage, at each age between 20 and 80. Estimates are provided by OACT in five-year age ranges, explaining the shape of the lines.

age of the retiree, including the costs of dependents.[13] The total shown in the figure is summed over inpatient, outpatient, and pharmaceutical direct care; inpatient, outpatient, and pharmaceutical purchased care; and the US Family Health Plan. We estimated health care costs for five-year age groups, which explains the level spending between ages and jumps at five-year intervals. The medical retiree line begins at age 20, reflecting the minimum age at which a medical retiree can exit the service and begin receiving health care benefits. The career retiree line begins at 40, the minimum age at which an active-component enlistee will reach 20 YOS. The costs fluctuate over time, reflecting both the retiree's health care consumption and the variation in the presence of spouses and dependents. Recall that these estimates are the total health care costs to DoD from the sponsoring member, including any covered family members. Although we might expect medical retirees to consume more health care for themselves, there could be differences in family coverage and consumption, as well as supplement medical insurance use, between the two groups.

It is striking, however, that health care for a medical retiree drops so much between peak consumption at age 40 and Medicare eligibility at age 65, from $9,000 to $6,000 per year. OACT calculates average consumption based on *current* users, reflecting the

---

[13] Under-65 health care cost estimates are from the financial statement memo accompanying the FY 2015 MERHCF report (OACT, 2017, pp. 16–30), and over-65 cost estimates are from the MERHCF valuation report (OACT, 2016b, Table E3).

health consumption patterns of prior, rather than future, cohorts. The MERHCF report notes that medical retirees are less likely than career retirees to live near DoD health care facilities and that career retirees often plan retirement so that they can live near such facilities. Given that this could change, and that future cohorts of medical retirees might continue to use TRICARE at higher rates than past cohorts did between the ages of 40 and 65, we performed robustness checks of the model in which we projected costs to DoD related to changes in accession medical standards under different health care consumption patterns, higher than what is shown in Figure 4.7. Finally, we should note that the costs to DoD change not only by usage of TRICARE facilities but also by the retiree's age and Medicare eligibility. Care provided by DoD to Medicare-eligible people is reimbursed by the MERHCF. We did not attempt to examine the reimbursement system in detail.

Figure 4.8 shows the lifetime health care costs for medical and career retirees at the age of retirement—in effect, adding each future year's average cost and adjusting it for changes in medical costs over the course of the retiree's life expectancy.[14] In addition, rather than adjusting a fixed payment growing at certain rate, we adjusted the

Figure 4.8
Expected Lifetime Health Care Costs for Retirees

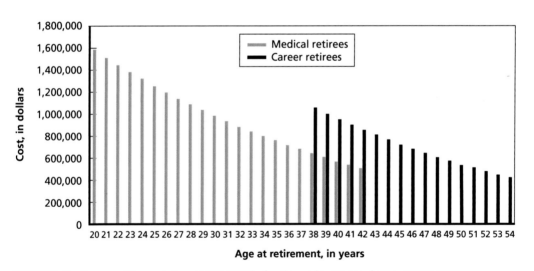

SOURCES: For the over-65 population, OACT, 2016b; for the under-65 population, OACT, 2017.
NOTE: The figure shows the lifetime costs per retiree for health care, including dependent coverage, based on the age at retirement. The lifetime costs are the net present value of summed costs at each age. Life expectancies differ between medical and career retirees.

---

[14] As noted, per OACT, life expectancy for a medical retiree is 76 and for a career retiree is 80; we assumed 2.75-percent inflation and a 5.5-percent long-term trend in growth in the cost of medical care.

age–cost vectors in Figure 4.7 to calculate the expected cost of health *at each age* based on the retiree's initial age.[15]

Unlike cash benefits, which are higher among career retirees, lifetime health costs are much higher for medical retirees, by virtue of the fact that medical costs grow at a faster rate than inflation (5.5 percent, compared with the assumed 2.75-percent inflation). Because the growth in costs accumulates over time, the difference between one year of lifetime benefits is not the same as the difference in one year of health care costs.

In sum, we calculated, for each YOS, the present value to DoD of the lifetime cash benefits and health care that an exiting service member would receive. We needed to make one final discount to complete our per-recruit expected cost estimate. The vector of costs that we calculated is expressed in present-value terms. For example, the present value of the lifetime cash benefits to a disabled service member who medically retires in the first YOS is $299,700 (the first blue bar in Figure 4.6), but the present value of the same benefits to a disabled service member who medically retires in the 19th YOS is $668,584 (the last blue bar in Figure 4.6). The difference reflects that the initial monthly benefit is based on completed YOS, so the first-year retiree has a cost of $847 per month and the 19th-year retiree has a cost of $2,379 per month. However, those comparisons require the assumption that both retirees medically retired at the same time. In other words, $299,700 and $668,584 are the costs today of two retirees who have 0 and 18 completed YOS, respectively. Our model is based on a per-recruit expected value, rather than comparing successive cohorts. We had to take into account that, if a service member retires with 18 years of completed service, 18 years of inflation and discounting have accrued since the first YOS. Hence, our final discount was to put all of the cost estimates in terms of the value at year 0; the $668,584 today is worth $266,169 in 18 years.

A summary of the probability and cost estimates, as well as the model's structure, is shown in Table 4.1, where each cell has two values: the probability of flowing to that state in that YOS (Pr) and the cost of that state and YOS (C). The sum of all the probabilities in each column set and each row is 1. In the first three sets of columns (death, officer, and reserve), the probability is fixed, so there is no cost estimate. The next three sets of columns (nonmedical separation, medical separation, and medical retirement) have positive probabilities only in YOS 0–18; afterward, an enlistee is eli-

---

[15] Specifically, the lump sum of the cash benefits can be expressed as a geometric series relating the initial benefit, B, to the growth rate in benefits, g, and the discount rate, r. But, for health benefits, B changes every year based on the retiree's age, so the series must be calculated by hand to take into account the growth in the amount spent on benefits every year.

Table 4.1
A Model Matrix of Probability and Cost for Each State in Each Year

YOS	Death	Officer	Reserve	Nonmedical Separation	Medical Separation	Medical Retirement	Career Retirement	AC Enlistee (Stock)
0	(pr, —)	(pr, —)	(pr, —)	(pr, $0)	(pr, C)	(pr, C)	(0, —)	(pr, $0)
1	(pr, —)	(pr, —)	(pr, —)	(pr, $0)	(pr, C)	(pr, C)	(0, —)	(pr, $0)
2	(pr, —)	(pr, —)	(pr, —)	(pr, $0)	(pr, C)	(pr, C)	(0, —)	(pr, $0)
3	(pr, —)	(pr, —)	(pr, —)	(pr, $0)	(pr, C)	(pr, C)	(0, —)	(pr, $0)
4	(pr, —)	(pr, —)	(pr, —)	(pr, $0)	(pr, C)	(pr, C)	(0, —)	(pr, $0)
5	(pr, —)	(pr, —)	(pr, —)	(pr, $0)	(pr, C)	(pr, C)	(0, —)	(pr, $0)
6	(pr, —)	(pr, —)	(pr, —)	(pr, $0)	(pr, C)	(pr, C)	(0, —)	(pr, $0)
7	(pr, —)	(pr, —)	(pr, —)	(pr, $0)	(pr, C)	(pr, C)	(0, —)	(pr, $0)
8	(pr, —)	(pr, —)	(pr, —)	(pr, $0)	(pr, C)	(pr, C)	(0, —)	(pr, $0)
9	(pr, —)	(pr, —)	(pr, —)	(pr, $0)	(pr, C)	(pr, C)	(0, —)	(pr, $0)
10	(pr, —)	(pr, —)	(pr, —)	(pr, $0)	(pr, C)	(pr, C)	(0, —)	(pr, $0)
11	(pr, —)	(pr, —)	(pr, —)	(pr, $0)	(pr, C)	(pr, C)	(0, —)	(pr, $0)
12	(pr, —)	(pr, —)	(pr, —)	(pr, $0)	(pr, C)	(pr, C)	(0, —)	(pr, $0)
13	(pr, —)	(pr, —)	(pr, —)	(pr, $0)	(pr, C)	(pr, C)	(0, —)	(pr, $0)
14	(pr, —)	(pr, —)	(pr, —)	(pr, $0)	(pr, C)	(pr, C)	(0, —)	(pr, $0)
15	(pr, —)	(pr, —)	(pr, —)	(pr, $0)	(pr, C)	(pr, C)	(0, —)	(pr, $0)
16	(pr, —)	(pr, —)	(pr, —)	(pr, $0)	(pr, C)	(pr, C)	(0, —)	(pr, $0)
17	(pr, —)	(pr, —)	(pr, —)	(pr, $0)	(pr, C)	(pr, C)	(0, —)	(pr, $0)
18	(pr, —)	(pr, —)	(pr, —)	(pr, $0)	(pr, C)	(pr, C)	(0, —)	(pr, $0)
19	(pr, —)	(pr, —)	(pr, —)	(0, —)	(0, —)	(0, —)	(pr, C)	(pr, $0)

Table 4.1—Continued

YOS	Death	Officer	Reserve	Nonmedical Separation	Medical Separation	Medical Retirement	Career Retirement	AC Enlistee (Stock)
20	(pr, —)	(pr, —)	(pr, —)	(0, —)	(0, —)	(0, —)	(pr, C)	(pr, $0)
21	(pr, —)	(pr, —)	(pr, —)	(0, —)	(0, —)	(0, —)	(pr, C)	(pr, $0)
22	(pr, —)	(pr, —)	(pr, —)	(0, —)	(0, —)	(0, —)	(pr, C)	(pr, $0)
23	(pr, —)	(pr, —)	(pr, —)	(0, —)	(0, —)	(0, —)	(pr, C)	(pr, $0)
24	(pr, —)	(pr, —)	(pr, —)	(0, —)	(0, —)	(0, —)	(pr, C)	(pr, $0)
25	(pr, —)	(pr, —)	(pr, —)	(0, —)	(0, —)	(0, —)	(pr, C)	(pr, $0)
26	(pr, —)	(pr, —)	(pr, —)	(0, —)	(0, —)	(0, —)	(pr, C)	(pr, $0)
27	(pr, —)	(pr, —)	(pr, —)	(0, —)	(0, —)	(0, —)	(pr, C)	(pr, $0)
28	(pr, —)	(pr, —)	(pr, —)	(0, —)	(0, —)	(0, —)	(pr, C)	(pr, $0)
29	(pr, —)	(pr, —)	(pr, —)	(0, —)	(0, —)	(0, —)	(pr, C)	(pr, $0)
30	(pr, —)	(pr, —)	(pr, —)	(0, —)	(0, —)	(0, —)	(pr, C)	(pr, $0)
31	(pr, —)	(pr, —)	(pr, —)	(0, —)	(0, —)	(0, —)	(pr, C)	(pr, $0)
32	(pr, —)	(pr, —)	(pr, —)	(0, —)	(0, —)	(0, —)	(pr, C)	(pr, $0)
33	(pr, —)	(pr, —)	(pr, —)	(0, —)	(0, —)	(0, —)	(pr, C)	(pr, $0)
34	(pr, —)	(pr, —)	(pr, —)	(0, —)	(0, —)	(0, —)	(pr, C)	(0, $0)[a]

NOTE: This table represents a schematic of the weighted average used in the cost model: the probability of each exit method in each path (Pr) is multiplied by the expected post-service cost (C). The sum of all the probabilities in each column and each row is 1. In the first three columns (death, officer, and reserve), the probability is fixed, so there is no cost estimate. The next three columns (nonmedical separation, medical separation, and medical retirement) have positive probabilities only in YOS 0–18; afterward, an enlistee is eligible for career retirement. Gray = We fixed the probabilities between iterations of the model. A cost of "—" indicates that we did not calculate it because of fixed probability. $0 = We assumed the cost of that exit to be $0. C = a calculated, nonzero postservice cost that varies by YOS and type of exit. Red = The policy change alters the probability of medical retirement.

[a] Because the model ends here, we assume that no one can be retained as an AC enlistee beyond this year, so probability = 0.

gible for career retirement.[16] Hence, in the next column, career retirement has zero probability in years 0 through 18 but is positive afterward. Nonmedical separation and active-component enlistees have $0.00 in each state-by-year cost cell.

The table shows how a change to accession medical standards is evaluated in the model. The regression estimates from Chapter Three are incorporated into the probability of medical retirement in the first five YOS.

The model's calculation is straightforward. Each row of the probability–cost table is summed, then the row totals are summed into a single number. To calculate the cost of a policy change, we did this arithmetic twice, the first time using the baseline probabilities and costs, the second using the probabilities as a result of the policy change. The difference in the two total sums is the effect of the policy on expected cost. Our baseline estimate was $87,590; that is the expected postservice cost from our model (with its numerous assumptions) to DoD of a single recruit. We noted a dip in health care expenditures for medical retirees after age 40, as shown in Figure 4.7, and attributed it to cohort effects, such that we might expect future retirees to use their TRICARE benefits more than past retirees did. If we assumed that costs remained constant after age 40, rather than dropping, as the figure shows, the baseline estimate would be $89,848. We also assumed that the age of recruits in the first YOS was 19. If instead we assumed that it was 22, the baseline estimate would be $85,194. We give a precise dollar amount here to show the range across assumptions, but these estimates should not be interpreted precisely, nor as a budget equivalent, as mentioned previously.

Results

In Chapter Three, we examined the following policy changes and the probability of being medically discharged:

- 2004 abdominal (tightening) and asthma (loosening)
- 2005 knee (tightening), abdominal (tightening), hearing (tightening), skin and cellular (tightening), and endocrine (tightening)
- 2010 elbow (tightening), skin and cellular (loosening), and orthotics (loosening).

Although we can estimate the 2004 and 2005 policy changes' effect on the probability of medical retirement in the first eight YOS, the effect of the 2010 changes can be measured only through the first five years. For easy comparability of cost estimates, we show only the five-year estimates. The effects of each policy (Figure 3.7) must be

---

[16] It is technically possible for an enlistee to medically retire when eligible for career retirement; we relaxed the assumption of career retirement at 20 YOS in sensitivity analyses of the model.

We express YOS as completed YOS, rather than standard YOS. For example, the first YOS is 1, equivalent to 0 completed YOS. A service member becomes eligible for retirement after 19 completed YOS (the 20th year).

incorporated into the cost model. There are several ways to do this, based on how the cumulative probability estimated via the regressions is transposed to single-YOS probability. For example, the 2005 change to the accession medical policy on knee extension resulted in an estimated decrease in the probability of medical retirement of 0.07 percentage points by year 5 for the Army. But as shown in Table 4.1, the cost model requires a change in probability in *each year 1 through 5*, not just cumulatively by year 5. The model presented in Chapter Three can produce estimates after three YOS, four years, and five years. Because of the small number of service members medically discharged in the first two YOS, the model cannot estimate those effects. We used three-, four-, and five-year effects to populate our cost model. The method we used to distribute the estimated effects across YOS affected our cost estimates. To be transparent about the sensitivity of our results to the specification, we developed the model to accommodate three "shapes" of the probability vector. Figure 4.9 summarizes our shapes.

The black markers in the third, fourth, and fifth YOS are the regression coefficients from the analysis presented in Chapter Three, with the mark at –0.00070 representing the five-year cumulative decrease in the probability of medically retiring. Each shape shows how the probability decrease can look in each year if the annual probability is nonzero only in the years our model can estimate, years 3 through 5 (shape 1); if the first two years' probabilities are linearly interpolated from the third year (shape 2); or if each year's probability is linearly interpolated from the final cumulative prob-

Figure 4.9
Cumulative Distribution Function of Probability Changes in Three Interpolation Scenarios

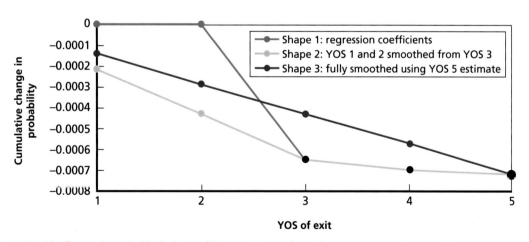

NOTE: The figure shows in black the coefficient estimates from the regression analysis. Each line represents a means of interpolating five years of probability changes from the three estimates given, the three-, four-, and five-year regression coefficients from Chapter Three (shape 1), years 1 and 2 smoothed using the year 3 estimate from Chapter Three (shape 2), and fully smoothed using the five-year estimate from Chapter Three (shape 3).

ability (shape 3). Although the differences between shapes are small, the difference between exiting in the first versus third YOS can have large lifetime costs. If we use only the given estimates (shape 1), the cost estimate could be biased downward. For that reason, and to take advantage of estimates we were able to produce for YOS 3–5, we treated shape 2 as our baseline. The other shapes, along with assumptions described earlier regarding age at first YOS and, for those serving for a career before retiring, YOS at exit, can serve as sensitivity analysis and allow us to create ranges for our cost estimates.[17]

The probability and cost estimates that are built into the model are based on service-wide DoD estimates. Service-specific estimates were not available. The accession medical policies, however, were service specific. To provide cost estimates, we applied the DoD model to the service policies. Note that, to the extent that services vary in the YOS distribution for a given exit type, such as voluntary separation or medical discharge, our cost estimate would also vary. To gain some insight into this, we considered a 2017 study on military retirement accrual charges that simulated service-specific accrual charges for retirement benefits (Hosek, Asch, and Mattock, 2017). The authors estimated that, for active-component enlistees, the Army, Navy, and Marine Corps accrual rates would be lower than the current single DoD accrual charge, and the Air Force's would be higher. Hence, our costs estimates for service-specific policy changes might be overstating the costs to the Army, Navy, and Marine Corps but understating the costs to the Air Force.

We now present our estimates of the postservice costs associated with the changes to accession medical policies that we analyzed in Chapter Two. For the purposes of illustration, we describe how we derived our estimate using the tightening of the knee standard in 2005. Recall that the effect that tightening the knee standard had on disability retirements was statistically significant for the Army, Marine Corps, and Navy. We repeat those results in the first row of Table 4.2. As discussed previously in this section, the status quo expected postservice cost per recruit is $87,590. Because the knee policy was associated with a reduction in disability retirements, and therefore an increase in the probability of exiting through other states, we estimated that the expected cost per recruit would decrease under the new policy. The amount of the reduction varied by service because the size of the policy's effect differs. To put the per-recruit change in expected cost into perspective, we scaled to 10,000 service members.[18] The final line of Table 4.2 shows the percentage reduction in our per-recruit cost

---

[17] The range of estimates produced using each policy shape, starting age, and retirement age is presented for each policy in Table E.1 in Appendix E.

[18] Alternatively, we could have scaled the results by the size of the accession cohort in the year of the policy change. For instance, in 2005, the accession cohorts were 63,324 (Army), 32,015 (Marine Corps), 37,729 (Navy), and 19,092 (Air Force) (OUSD[P&R], 2005, Table B-1). Doing so would have combined the size of the effect with the size of the cohort, and our intent was to isolate the size of the policy effect. Therefore, we scaled the per-recruit cost by the same number across services and years.

Table 4.2
Potential Postservice Costs Associated with the Tightening of the Knee Policy, 2005, per 10,000 Service Members

Change	Army	Marine Corps	Navy	Air Force
Five-year effect of the 2005 tightening of the knee policy (percentage points)	−0.07	−0.04	−0.02	—
Status quo expected cost per recruit, in dollars	87,590	87,590	87,590	
Per-recruit expected cost associated with tightening the knee policy, in dollars	87,157	87,378	87,487	
Change in expected costs per recruit, in dollars	−433	−212	−103	
Change in expected cost per 10,000 recruits (rounded), in dollars	−4,333,000	−2,124,000	−1,027,000	
Percentage change in baseline cost	−0.49	−0.24	−0.11	

NOTE: The numbers in this table represent the findings of the cost analysis model and show, in stages, how the per-recruit change in expected retirement cost could be scaled by accession cohorts of various sizes by providing a 10,000–service member estimate. The expected costs per recruit are rounded, and the final change in expected cost per 10,000 recruits is rounded to the nearest thousand. The status quo expected postservice cost per recruit is $87,590; it is based on an average of the expected postservice cost for each type of exit from the active component in each YOS, weighted by the probability of exit. The probabilities are based on estimates from OACT, and the model permutes the probability of medical retirement, resulting in the per-recruit change. We express costs in present-value terms; they represent the value of a lifetime of benefits discounted back to the first YOS.

estimate associated with tightening of the knee policy in 2005. That is, we expect the postservice DoD cost of a recruit to decrease by 0.11 to 0.49 percent.

Under different assumptions, our baseline estimate for the Army of a per-recruit decline of $433 would change. The model assumes that the age of enlistment is 19, but if we assume that the age of enlistment is 22, the cost saving is smaller, a decline of $422. The difference is due to the number of years of benefits a medical retiree would receive. In addition, we noted that the current dip in health care costs after age 40, shown in Figure 4.7, is not likely to be sustained in the future. If we assume instead constant health care costs between age 40 and 65, essentially removing the dip, the effect of the policy is larger—a savings of $458. In other words, the more expensive we assume health care to be, the larger the potential savings from a decrease in the number of retirements.

Using the same methodology shown in Table 4.2, we were able to similarly estimate the change in postservice costs associated with the size of the other policy changes analyzed throughout this study. Because our model does not follow a particular accession cohort over time and rather should be thought of as the estimated per-recruit cost, with its many assumptions, we scaled our results by 10,000 to give an idea of how small per-recruit savings in the hundreds of dollars could quickly scale. Table 4.3 summarizes our cost estimates for all effects that are significant at the 1- or 5-percent level (from Figure 3.7 in Chapter Three), again assuming that age at accession is 19, career retirement exit occurs at 19 YOS, and shape 2 from above, in which the first two years' probability are linearly interpolated from the third year. We also show the percentage change in baseline costs. Cost estimates produced by varying these assumptions can be found in Table E.1 in Appendix E.

During the regression analysis described in Chapter Three, we estimated that the probability of medically retiring is lower if accession medical standards are tighter. The cost model in this chapter uses the postservice cost of a recruit to estimate how large the potential cost savings of that reduction could be, given the large costs associated with medical retirement. The estimates presented in Table 4.3 apply the regression analysis results to the potential costs and then scale them by 10,000. The key takeaway from the table is not the dollar amount, given that it does not represent the actual amount saved, but the direction of the cost changes and the relative percentages. Tighter accession standards reduced the expected postservice costs to DoD through a lower probability of medical discharge.

Caveats and Limitations of the Cost Analysis

As stated previously, the cost analysis presented in this chapter was not a budgetary estimate of cost savings but a notional model of the magnitude of costs associated with a reduction in the probability of medical discharge. A reduction in postservice costs presented here should not be interpreted as money freed in the DoD budget to be spent elsewhere. The reason it cannot be interpreted that way is the assumptions used to produce the estimates—specifically, the numerous costs not included to DoD and other agencies. Instead, this model is an estimate of the postservice obligations that DoD pays out to career retirees, medical retirees, and medical separatees and a way to show the magnitude of the impact that accession medical policy changes have on those postservice obligations.

There are other possible, potentially more-straightforward, approaches to estimating costs associated with changes to accession medical standards that we did not pursue. First, we did not sum up the transactional costs to implementing a change to accession medical policy: the number of screenings, waivers, or disability evaluations and the costs per screening, per waiver, and per evaluation. Most of these costs are fixed for the facility and staff that perform the action and not itemizable by policy change.

Second, we did not follow the cohorts who joined right after each policy change and track their exits, primarily because they had not served for enough years to reach each possible exit type. We could have applied exit probabilities to the years served and made assumptions about future retirement patterns, or we could have applied the exit

Table 4.3
Cost Estimates and Percentage Change in Cost Relative to the Baseline, Associated with Accession Medical Standard Changes in the First Five Years of Service, per 10,000 Service Members

Condition	Change	Army		Marine Corps		Navy		Air Force	
		Amount, in Dollars	Percentage	Amount, in Dollars	Percentage	Amount, in Dollars	Percentage	Amount, in Dollars	Percentage
2004									
Abdominal	Tightened			−4,809,000	−0.55	−1,495,000	−0.17		
2005									
Knee	Tightened	−4,333,000	−0.49	−2,124,000	−0.24	−1,027,000	−0.11		
Abdominal	Tightened			−1,902,000	−0.22	−1,657,000	−0.19	−1,514,000	−0.17
Skin and cellular	Tightened	−8,938,000	−1.02	−3,227,000	−0.37	−1,936,000	−0.22		
Endocrine	Tightened			−2,189,000	−0.25				
2010									
Elbow	Tightened	−3,017,000	−0.34	−3,852,000	−0.44	−1,666,000	−0.19	−3,249,000	−0.37

NOTE: The numbers in this table represent the expected retirement cost changes associated with each policy change, given the regression estimates of the change in the five-year medical discharge rate, or the percentage of the cohort who have been medically discharged by the end of the fifth YOS. Per-recruit cost estimates are scaled by 10,000. The second number in each pair of rows is the percentage change in cost from the baseline. The model used to generate these estimates assumes that the cost to DoD when the active-component enlistee becomes an officer, becomes a reservist, dies, or separates through a channel other than disability evaluation is 0. Costs of medical retirement, medical separation, and career retirement include the lifetime cash compensation and health care benefits discounted back to the first YOS. We provide a cost estimate only if the relationship between accession medical standards and disability outcomes (the findings from Chapter Three) were significant at the 1- or 5-percent level. Dollar amounts are rounded to the nearest thousand.

probabilities to earlier accession cohorts who had served longer. We did not take either of these approaches because (1) cohorts vary over time in composition and experience, (2) it is critical that the results from our cost exercise be driven by changes in the probability of various exits and not by composition or experience, and (3) these approaches would have required us to abandon certain assumptions that make the model tractable (e.g., assumptions about survivor benefits or retention costs) and make assumptions that make the model less applicable (e.g., previous cohorts had different service experiences, such as deployments, or different health care needs). Given these challenges, we elected to scale per-recruit costs according to a fixed number (10,000) of service members rather than following members of a cohort through their careers.

Similarly, we did not count up the number of service members affected by the policy change and sum their pay and benefits, whether observed or estimated. If we found that, as a result of a change to accession standards, 50 more service members had medically retired, one approach would have been to calculate how much a medical retirement costs, multiply that amount by 50, and conclude that that was the cost associated with the policy. But this assumes that the exit states other than disability retirement, whether that be voluntary separation after a single term or retirement after 20 or more YOS, are costless, and that is not always true. Moreover, a count of affected recruits is not applicable across cohorts or services, which can be differently sized. And finally, it would misrepresent the findings of our regression analysis, which was a change to the *probability of medical discharge*, not an absolute number of service members.

In addition, our model reflects current retiree policy and benefit design. If the cost, eligibility, or use of TRICARE or the generosity or structure of retiree payments change in the future, these estimates will change. In particular, this analysis calculates retirement payments according to the old retirement system. It does not take into account the reformed retirement program, which features increased portability, a smaller defined benefit, the end of cliff vesting, and lower costs to both DoD and the Treasury (see Asch, Mattock, and Hosek, 2015).

As mentioned previously, our baseline throughout this report has been the effect that accession medical policies have on medical retirements, primarily because they represent two-thirds of all medical discharges and because of data limitations in our cost model (OACT provides exit probabilities for medical retirement, but we had to manually estimate the proportion of all withdrawals that are medical separations, based on the observed proportions in the data). Because the effect that accession medical standards have on retirement outcomes is much stronger than that on medical separations, by applying retirement estimates to all discharges in the cost model, we overstated the effect on medical separations. However, the cost of medical separation to DoD is trivial relative to the cost of medical retirements, so we believe that this has only a minor impact on our results.

Finally, as shown in Figures 4.2 and 4.3, approximately half of medical retirements occur in the first five YOS, and half occur later. Our baseline estimates from Chapter Two, used to produce cost estimates in this chapter, represent changes in the probability of medical retirement through the first five YOS. Therefore, the estimates presented in this chapter capture changes in postservice costs to DoD for only half of all medical retirements, specifically those that occur early in the career.

CHAPTER FIVE

Conclusions

In this study, we examined the effects that changes to accession medical standards have on disability outcomes for service members who were subject to medical examinations right before and right after policy changes. We also estimated the costs that DoD incurs when service members are medically separated or retired from active-component enlisted service.

During our review of accession medical standards, we identified ten changes to policy that mapped to a sufficient number of medical discharges to be able to estimate an effect:

- 2004
  - abdominal, tightening: "history of" gastrointestinal bleeding added as a disqualifying condition, and conditions added to the hernia standard
  - asthma, loosening: changed from diagnosed at any age to diagnosed after the 13th birthday
- 2005
  - knee, tightening: knee-flexion requirement changed from 90 degrees to 110 degrees, and other conditions added as disqualifying
  - abdominal, tightening: addition of and changes to criteria for several conditions
  - hearing, tightening: audiometric hearing thresholds changed from "both ears" to "either ear," and use of hearing aids added as a disqualifying condition
  - skin and cellular, tightening: any degree (rather than just mild) of psoriasis considered disqualifying, and "current or history of" added to several conditions
  - endocrine, tightening: "current or history of" added to several conditions, and pituitary dysfunction added as a disqualifying condition
- 2010
  - elbow, tightening: increased flexion requirement for the elbow, from 100 degrees to 130 degrees, and "current" removed for some conditions

- skin and cellular, loosening: atopic dermatitis changed from after the 9th birthday to after the 12th birthday
- orthotics, loosening: removal of reference to orthotics as a disqualifying condition.

Accession Medical Standards and Disability Outcomes

We found no effect on medical discharges for the three policies that were loosened: asthma in 2004, orthotics in 2010, and skin and cellular in 2010. However, for six of the other seven accession medical standards that were tightened, we found statistically significant reductions in medical retirements for one or more services; the seventh, a tightening of the hearing standard in 2005, was correlated with a reduced probability of medical discharge, unconditional on disability rating. Marine Corps results were most sensitive to tightened standards, consistently generating statistically significant reductions in medical retirements. When we restricted our evaluation to medical separations, we found small effects that were rarely statistically significant, indicating that the primary impact of changes in accession medical standard is on discharges with disability ratings of at least 30 percent. The results of our baseline model—disability retirements through the first five YOS—are consistent under a variety of other specifications, including five-year estimates for any disability rating and eight-year effects for any disability rating or only ratings 30 percent or higher.

Postservice Costs to the Department of Defense

In addition to estimating disability outcomes resulting from changes in accession medical standards, we developed a model to translate these effects into estimates of the cost (or savings) DoD incurs—through changes in the likelihood of medical discharge—when an active-component enlistee completes military service. Our model assumes that, during each year of service, an active-component enlistee could medically retire, medically separate, complete a career (20 or more YOS) and retire, become an officer, become a reservist, die, voluntarily or involuntarily separate, or remain an active-component enlistee—and assigns probabilities and costs for each of these potential outcomes. When the probability of being medically discharged decreases, for instance, other probabilities must increase.[1]

We estimated the cost to DoD for postservice, assuming that an active-component enlistee does not become an officer, join the reserves after separating voluntarily, or die. DoD pays cash benefits and the cost of health care for life when an active-component

---

[1]   That is, the probabilities must sum to 1. If one decreases, one or more of the others must increase.

enlistee retires, either medically or after 20 or more YOS. In addition, a service member who medically retires with a disability rating of less than 30 percent receives a lump-sum cash payment and six months of health care benefits.

Using costs and probabilities from OACT, we estimated that the baseline per-recruit postservice cost to DoD for an active-component enlistee is $87,590. The interpretation of this is that, when an active-component enlistee joins the active-component enlistee ranks, and the time they will spend in service and how they will leave is unknown, the expected cost to DoD once they leave service is $87,590. The vast majority of active-component enlistees complete less than 20 YOS and are not medically retired, thereby not costing DoD anything. However, for the nearly 20 percent who do retire after 20 years or who are medically retired, the lifetime costs are close to $2 million per person, resulting in a weighted average as calculated above.

We then varied the probabilities of the different ways a service member can leave military service based on the estimates of the effect that accession medical standards have on medical discharge. For each statistically significant effect, we recalculated the per-recruit postservice cost to DoD and then scaled the difference by 10,000 service members. For large effects, such as skin and cellular policy changes in the Army in 2005, the cost savings to DoD could reach $9 million per 10,000 service members. In general, the estimates vary, from –$1 million to –$5 million per 10,000 service members (that is, savings of $1 million to $5 million).

These cost estimates reflect only the costs to DoD, and they are discounted back to the year of discharge. They do not include costs to other departments, such as VA. They also do not capture the costs associated with replacing potential recruits who fail to meet a stricter accession standard. They provide a notional estimate of the magnitude of costs associated with a reduction in the probability of medical discharge, not as a budgetary estimate of cost savings that can be reappropriated by Congress or the Comptroller General for other activities.

Implications for the Future

The model we developed in this study to measure the effects of policy changes on disability outcomes is built at the person-year level. To use it to estimate how future changes to accession medical standards might affect disability outcomes, we would need to be able to populate all of the characteristics of the model, including deployment experiences, pay grade, occupation, and demographic characteristics, for everyone who will serve in the military in the future. We would also need to predict how a future change in the standard would differ in its relationship to injury or illness. It is not possible to do this, so the model as built cannot predict disability effects that result from future policy changes.

However, patterns in our estimates indicate what service and individual characteristics are associated with disability outcomes. Higher BMI was generally correlated with higher rates of disability outcomes. Deployments had mixed effects on disability outcomes. Members who had ever deployed were more likely to be medically discharged than those who never deployed, which is consistent with the idea that deployments are physically demanding and can result in injuries that affect one's ability to continue serving. On the other hand, service members who deployed more (e.g., more deployment spells, more total months deployed) were less likely to be medically discharged. This is likely a selection effect: Those who are healthy, and therefore less likely to be referred for disability evaluation, are those who can tolerate multiple or long deployment events. Other variables, such as pay grade and occupation, were consistently significant in our regressions, but their patterns varied by policy tested.

Taken together, these results suggest that individual and service characteristics are correlated with medical discharges, even in the absence of changes to accession medical standards. But after controlling for several observable characteristics, we found that the medical standards to which a service member is held at the time of MEPS processing do influence the probability of being medically discharged. Holding recruits to higher standards reduces the likelihood that they will experience injuries and illnesses that will render them unable to serve, but there are also costs associated with stricter standards (not captured empirically in this study), including the recruiting costs associated with replacing potential recruits who are disqualified on the basis of medical standards.

Additional Details of the Policy Review

To evaluate whether policies were tightened or loosened, we used document-comparison functions in Microsoft Word and Adobe Acrobat programs to identify every change that occurred when each revision of DoDI 6130.03 was issued. We evaluated text changes for their meaning and in the context of the overall intent of the standard. When a new disqualifying condition was added to a body system category, this was interpreted as a tightening because the new condition expands the range of conditions for which someone can be medically disqualified. Similarly, when conditions were deleted, this was interpreted as a loosening. When a criterion by which a medical condition or functionality of a body part or system is evaluated was changed, we determined what the criteria change meant for an individual physically and then classified the change accordingly.

For example, when the range-of-motion standard was changed for the knee from "full extension compared with contralateral" and "flexion to 90 degrees" to "full extension to 0 degrees" and "flexion to 110 degrees," we determined that both changes were a tightening of standards because the criteria are more restrictive (i.e., to be medically qualified, one now needed a greater range of motion in the knee than previously). Another criterion change example is the asthma standard: Prior to 2004, asthma diagnosed at any age was disqualifying. In 2004, the standard was changed to "diagnosed and symptomatic after the 13th birthday." This means that someone with childhood asthma that resolved before the 13th birthday would have previously been medically disqualified but now could be considered for accession, enlistment, and induction. This was interpreted as a loosening.

For minor wording changes, such as adding the word "current" or "history of," we had to determine what the previous standard was and then determine whether the minor wording change changed the intent of the standard or the criteria for the condition. For example, if the standard previously just listed the condition and the wording was changed to "current or history of," we interpreted this as no change because the criteria by which the condition is evaluated are still the same. However, if the standard previously just listed the condition and "current" was added, we interpreted this as a loosening because only potential enlistees with the condition currently would be medically disqualified, whereas, previously, the standard might have medically disqualified a potential enlistee with a history of the condition.

Table A.1 lists DoD and service-specific policy documents that govern medical standards. Table A.2 lists DoD and service-specific policy documents that govern physical standards. In Chapter Two, we presented a summary of the ten policy changes that we have enough outcomes to have analyzed throughout this study. Table A.3 contains a more complete list of changes to medical standards during that period, by body system. In that table, we indicate those policy changes that we tested.

Table A.1
Medical Standard Policy Documents

Issuing Organization	Accession	Disability	Retention	Deployability
DoD	DoDI 6130.03; DoDI 1304.26	DoDI 1332.14; DoDI 1332.30	DoDI 1332.14; DoDI 1332.30; DoD Directive 6040.41	DoDI 6490.07
Army	AR 40-501	AR 40-501	AR 40-501	AR 40-501
Navy	NAVMED P-117, Chapter 15	SECNAVINST 1850.4E; SECNAVINST 6120.3; NAVMED P-117, Chapter 18	SECNAVINST 1850.4E; NAVMED P-117, Chapter 18; SECNAVINST 6120.3	SECNAVINST 1850.4E
Marine Corps	NAVMED P117, Chapter 15; MCO 1130.76D; Marine Corps Recruiting Command Order 1100.1	SECNAVINST 1850.4E; SECNAVINST 6120.3; NAVMED P-117, Chapter 18; MCO 1900.16	SECNAVINST 1850.4E; NAVMED P-117, Chapter 18; SECNAVINST 6120.3; MCO 1900.16	SECNAVINST 1850.4E; MCO 1900.16
Air Force	AFI 48-123; AFI 36-2002	AFI 48-123; AFI 44-157	AFI 48-123; AFI 36-3212	AFI 48-123; AFI 48-122

SOURCES: OUSD(P&R), 2010a, 2010b, 2011, 2017, 2018a, 2018b; Office of the Assistant Secretary of Defense for Health Affairs, 2004b; Headquarters, Department of the Army, 2017b; NAVMED, 2018a; Secretary of the Navy, 2002, 2009; Commandant of the Marine Corps, 2015, 2017; Commanding General, Marine Corps Recruiting Command, 2011; Director of Medical Operations and Research, Surgeon General, Headquarters, U.S. Air Force, 2018; Deputy Chief of Staff of the Air Force for Manpower, Personnel and Services, Accession and Training Management Division, 2017; Air Force Research Oversight and Compliance, 2000; Directorate of Personnel Services, Air Force's Personnel Center, 2009; U.S. Air Force Surgeon General, 2017.

NOTE: SECNAVINST = Secretary of the Navy instruction. MCO = Marine Corps order.

Table A.2
Physical Standard Policy Documents

Issuing Organization	Accession	Retention
DoD	DoDI 1308.3; DoDI 1304.26	DoDI 1308.3
Army	AR 40-501; AR 600-9	AR 40-501; AR 600-9; AR 635-40
Navy	Office of the Chief of Naval Operations Instruction 6110.1H; NAVMED P-117, Chapter 15	Office of the Chief of Naval Operations Instruction 6110.1H; SECNAVINST 6120.3
Marine Corps	NAVMED P-117, Chapter 15; MCO P1100.72C	SECNAVINST 1850.4E; SECNAVINST 6120.3; MCO 6110.3
Air Force	AFI 48-123	AFI 36-2905; AFI 48-123

SOURCES: Assistant Secretary of Defense for Force Management Policy, 2002; OUSD(P&R), 2017; Headquarters, Department of the Army, 2013, 2017a, 2017b; Office of the Chief of Naval Operations, Department of the Navy, 2005; Secretary of the Navy, 2002, 2009; Commandant of the Marine Corps, 2004, 2008; Director of Medical Operations and Research, Surgeon General, Headquarters, U.S. Air Force, 2018; Directorate of Personnel Services, Air Force's Personnel Center, 2015.

Table A.3
Summary of Major Condition Changes

Body System	Type of Change	2004	2005	2010	2011
Learning, psychiatric, and behavioral	Tightening		Added learning, psychiatric, and behavioral disorders (e.g., anxiety and PTSD)	Added conduct and personality disorders; added prior psychiatric hospitalization for any cause	
		Changed criteria for academic skill defects (specified attention-deficit disorder and ADHD and medication usage)		Changed criteria for ADHD	
	Loosening		Deleted conduct, personality, and behavioral disorders	Changed criteria for learning disorders, depression, and anxiety	
Abdominal organs and gastrointestinal system	Tightening	Added gastrointestinal bleed[a], added other abdominal hernia category[a]	Added GERD[a]; added history of surgery for peptic ulceration[a]; added metabolic liver disease[a]; added lactase deficiency	Changed criteria for inflammatory bowel disease by adding "current or history of" to the language[a], changed criteria for abdominal surgery from the preceding 60 days to the preceding six months[a], changed criteria for obesity surgery (added conditions that are disqualifying)	

Table A.3—Continued

Body System	Type of Change	2004	2005	2010	2011
Abdominal organs and gastrointestinal system, continued	Loosening		Changed criteria for gastritis (made current gastritis disqualifying if it requires maintenance medication); changed criteria for cholecystitis (made cholecystectomy not disqualifying if performed more than six months prior); changed criteria for splenectomy	Changed criteria for abdominal surgery (added that uncomplicated appendectomies meet the standards after three months)	Changed criteria for GERD; changed criteria for dyspepsia; changed criteria for gastric and duodenal ulcers
			Deleted congenital abnormalities of the stomach or duodenum		Deleted gastritis; deleted splenectomy
Endocrine and metabolic	Tightening		Added pituitary dysfunction[a]	Added metabolic syndrome beyond the 35th birthday; added dyslipidemia on medical management	Added metabolic bone disease; added male hypogonadism; added islet-cell tumors, nesidioblastosis, and hypoglycemia
			Changed criteria for several conditions (e.g., adrenal function, diabetes mellitus, hyperthyroidism, acromegaly) by adding "current or history of" to the language[a]		Changed criteria for diabetes mellitus disorders; changed criteria for pituitary dysfunction
	Loosening		Changed criteria for several conditions (e.g., goiter, hypothyroidism, thyroiditis, nutritional deficiencies) by adding "current" to the language		Changed criteria for adrenal dysfunction; changed criteria for goiter; changed criteria for hyperthyroidism

Table A.3—Continued

Body System	Type of Change	2004	2005	2010	2011
Hearing[b]	Tightening		Added the use of hearing aids[a]		
			Changed criteria for meeting hearing threshold levels from both ears to either ear[a]		
Lower extremities	Tightening		Added medial and lateral collateral ligament injuries[a]; added meniscal injuries[a]	Added stress fractures	
			Changed criteria for knee range of motion (changed extension requirement from "compared to contralateral" to "0 degrees" and flexion from "90 degrees" to "110 degrees")[a]; changed criteria for some conditions (e.g., deformities of the toes, clubfoot) by adding "current" where they previously included only a history of the condition[a]; changed criteria for pes planus (made a history of correction with orthotics disqualifying)	Changed criteria for plantar fasciitis by adding "or history of" to the language	

Table A.3—Continued

Body System	Type of Change	2004	2005	2010	2011
Lower extremities, continued	Loosening		Changed criteria for several conditions (e.g., pes planus, ingrown toenails, neuroma, loose or foreign body in the knee) by adding "current" to the language; changed criteria for leg length discrepancy (removed reference to it causing scoliosis)	Changed criteria for absence of a portion of a foot (added clarifying language for when met of a single lesser toe meets the standard); changed criteria for surgical reconstruction of knee ligaments (clarified when surgical correction met the standard; however, recurrent reconstruction of the anterior cruciate ligament was still disqualifying); changed criteria for meniscal repair (clarified when surgical correction met the standard); clarified language for hip dislocation (stated when hip dislocation met the standard)	
				Deleted orthotics[a]	

Table A.3—Continued

Body System	Type of Change	2004	2005	2010	2011
Lungs and chest	Tightening		Added specific reference to the types of acute lung infections that are disqualifying; changed criteria for several conditions (e.g., bronchiectasis, bronchopleural, bullous or generalized pulmonary emphysema) by adding "current or history of" to the language; added history of open or laparoscopic thoracic or chest wall (including breast) surgery in the preceding six months		
				Changed criteria for history of thoracic surgery (made all history disqualifying)	
	Loosening	Changed criteria for diagnosis of asthma (to diagnosed and symptomatic after 13th birthday)[a]; changed criteria for recurring cough, wheeze, or dyspnea (from "persists or recurs" for six months to more than 12 months)[a]	Changed criteria for several conditions (e.g., abnormal elevation of the diaphragm, abscess of lunch or mediastinum, chest wall malformations, pulmonary fibrosis, foreign body in lung) by adding "current" to the language	Changed criteria for asthma and reactive airway disease diagnosis (included criteria for how those with a history of the condition could still meet the standard); changed criteria for history of bronchiectasis	

Table A.3—Continued

Body System	Type of Change	2004	2005	2010	2011
Lungs and chest, continued	Loosening, continued	Deleted requirement for reversible airflow-obstruction test when asthma diagnosis is in question[a]	Deleted sarcoidosis; deleted silicone breast implants if less than 9 months since surgery or with symptomatic complications; deleted tuberculosis lesions		
Miscellaneous conditions of the extremities	Tightening		Added history of recurrent knee and shoulder instability; added bone or joint contusion	Added osteopenia; added history of cartilage surgery; added posttraumatic or exercise-induced compartment syndrome; added avascular necrosis of any bone; added tendon disorders	
				Clarified language for joint dislocation (specified subluxation in addition to instability); clarified language for orthopedic implants to correct abnormalities (included congenital and posttraumatic); changed criteria for osteochondritis dissecans by adding "or history of" to the language	

Table A.3—Continued

Body System	Type of Change	2004	2005	2010	2011
Miscellaneous conditions of the extremities, continued	Loosening		Changed criteria for several conditions (e.g., osteoporosis, osteomyelitis, osteochondritis dissecans) by adding "current" to the language	Changed criteria for bone or joint contusion and other injuries of more than minor in nature (from the preceding six weeks to the preceding six months); changed criteria for osteochondroma by adding "symptomatic" to the language	
Neurologic	Tightening		Added meningeal disorders, including cysts; added unconsciousness, amnesia, or disorientation of person, place, or time for 24 hours or longer postinjury; added Tourette's and tic disorders to chronic nervous system disorders	Added cerebrovascular conditions (e.g., stroke, vascular stenosis, transient ischemic attack); added Guillain-Barre syndrome; added syncope or atraumatic loss of consciousness	

Table A.3—Continued

Body System	Type of Change	2004	2005	2010	2011
Neurologic, continued	Tightening, continued		Changed criteria for congenital or acquired anomalies of the central nervous system (removed "if known to be progressive"); changed criteria for headaches by adding "or of such severity to require prescription medication"; changed criteria for posttraumatic seizures (epilepsy) from occurring more than one week after injury to more than 30 minutes after injury; changed criteria for skull fractures; changed criteria for persistent posttraumatic symptoms by adding "or have duration of greater than 1 month"	Changed criteria for headaches by adding more diagnoses and time conditions; changed criteria of head injury to include persistent vestibular, visual, or other focal neurologic defect; changed criteria for seizures (from epilepsy to any seizure)	
	Loosening		Deleted central nervous system shunts; deleted sleep apnea; deleted mood and anxiety disorders	Changed criteria for meningeal cysts (explicitly stated what met standards); changed criteria for amnesia (from 24 hours to seven days or longer) Deleted multiple skull or face fractures; deleted leptomeningeal cysts; deleted narcolepsy	
Rheumatologic[b]	Tightening				Added the category

Table A.3—Continued

Body System	Type of Change	2004	2005	2010	2011
Skin and cellular tissue, continued	Tightening			Added hidradenitis suppurativa; added prior burn injury involving 18 percent or more body surface area	
			Added scars that interfere with satisfactory performance or wearing of military clothinga; added current localized fungal infections		
			Changed criteria for several conditions (e.g., atopic and contact dermatitis, keloid formation, bullous dermatoses, hyperhidrosis of hands and feet, neurofibromatosis, radiodermatitis, scleroderma) by adding "current or history of" to the languagea; changed criteria psoriasis (made any psoriasis disqualifying, with no exceptions)[a]		
	Loosening		Changed criteria for atopic dermatitis (from after age 8 to after the 9th birthday)	Changed criteria for atopic dermatitis (from after the 9th birthday to after the 12th birthday)[a]; changed criteria for other nonspecific dermatitis (chronic and requiring more than treatment with over-the-counter medications)[a]; changed criteria for hyperhidrosis (unless controlled by topical medications); changed criteria for chronic urticaria	

Table A.3—Continued

Body System	Type of Change	2004	2005	2010	2011
Skin and cellular tissue	Loosening, continued		Deleted systemic fungal infections; deleted dermatitis factitial; deleted tattoos		
Spine and sacroiliac joints	Tightening		Added ankylosing spondylitis and inflammatory spondylopathies; added any surgical fusion as disqualifying		
			Changed criteria for sacroiliac joint pain and injury (made external support and limitation of physical activity disqualifying); changed criteria for conditions (e.g., vertebra dislocation or fracture, spina bifida, spondylolysis) by adding "current or history of"	Changed criteria for kyphosis and lordosis (from 55 degrees to 50 degrees)	
	Loosening			Changed criteria for lumbar scoliosis (from 20 degrees to 30 degrees); changed criteria for herniated disc (allowed certain surgical corrections)	

Table A.3—Continued

Body System	Type of Change	2004	2005	2010	2011
Upper extremities	Tightening		Added carpal tunnel and cubital tunnel syndromes; added lesion of ulnar and radial nerves		
			Changed criteria for residual weakness or injury in wrist, forearm, elbow, arm, or shoulder (removed grip strength measurements)	Changed criteria for elbow flexion (from 100 degrees to 130 degrees)[a]; changed criteria for several conditions (e.g., absence of fingers or portion of hand, polydactyly) by removing "current" from the language	
	Loosening		Changed criteria for several conditions (e.g., absence of fingers or portion of hand, polydactyly) by adding "current" to the language		
			Deleted scars and deformities of the fingers or hand		

a We tested this policy change.
b We omitted the "Loosening" row because we had no data for it.

APPENDIX B

Veterans Affairs Schedule for Rating Disabilities–Policy Crosswalk

To evaluate the potential effect that an accession medical standard policy change could have on disability outcomes, we needed to identify service members who were medically discharged with disabilities corresponding to the policy that changed. Table B.1 shows how we mapped policy changes to specific VASRD codes for the ten policy changes corresponding to a sufficient number of medical discharges to potentially detect an effect.

Table B.1
Veterans Affairs Schedule for Rating Disabilities Mappings for Select Accession Medical Standard Policy Changes

System	Our Name for the System	Direction	VASRD	VASRD Description
2004				
The digestive system	Abdominal	Tightening	5326[a]	Muscle hernia
			7205	Esophagus, diverticulum
			7304	Ulcer, gastric
			7305	Ulcer, duodenal
			7306	Ulcer, marginal
			7307	Gastritis, hypertrophic
			7310	Stomach, injury of, residuals
			7323	Colitis, ulcerative
			7324	Distomiasis, intestinal or hepatic
			7327	Diverticulitis
			7338	Hernia, inguinal
			7339	Hernia, ventral, postoperative
			7340	Hernia, femoral

Table B.1—Continued

System	Our Name for the System	Direction	VASRD	VASRD Description
The digestive system, continued	Abdominal, continued	Tightening, continued	7346	Hernia, hiatal
			7540[b]	Disseminated intravascular coagulation
The respiratory system: trachea and bronchi	Asthma	Loosening	6602	Asthma, bronchial
2005				
The musculoskeletal system: knee and leg	Knee	Tightening	5256	Knee, ankylosis
			5257	Knee, other impairment
			5258	Cartilage, semilunar, dislocated
			5313[c, d]	Group XIII function: extension of hip and flexion of knee
			5314[c]	Group XIV function: extension of knee[e]
The digestive system	Abdominal	Tightening	7203	Esophagus, stricture
			7204	Esophagus, spasm
			7205	Esophagus, diverticulum
			7304	Ulcer, gastric
			7305	Ulcer, duodenal
			7306	Ulcer, marginal
			7307	Gastritis, hypertrophic
			7318	Gall bladder, removal
			7323	Colitis, ulcerative
			7345	Liver disease, chronic, without cirrhosis
			7706[f]	Splenectomy
The ear	Hearing	Tightening	6200	Chronic suppurative otitis media
			6201	Chronic nonsuppurative otitis media
			6202	Otosclerosis
			6204	Peripheral vestibular disorders
			6205	Meniere's syndrome

Table B.1—Continued

System	Our Name for the System	Direction	VASRD	VASRD Description
The ear, continued	Hearing, continued	Tightening, continued	6207	Loss of auricle
			6208	Malignant neoplasm
			6209	Benign neoplasm
			6210	Chronic otitis externa
			6211	Tympanic membrane
			6260	Tinnitus, recurrent
The skin	Skin and cellular	Tightening	7800	Burn scar of the head, face, or neck; scar of the head, face, or neck due to other causes; or other disfigurement of the head, face, or neck
			7801	Burn scar or scar due to other causes, not of the head, face, or neck, that are deep and nonlinear
			7802	Burn scar or scar due to other causes, not of the head, face, or neck, that are superficial and nonlinear
			7804	Scar, unstable or painful
			7805	Scar, other
			7806	Dermatitis or eczema
			7816	Psoriasis
The endocrine system	Endocrine	Tightening	7901	Thyroid enlargement, toxic
			7902	Thyroid enlargement, nontoxic
			7903	Hypothyroidism
			7904	Hyperparathyroidism
			7905	Hypoparathyroidism
			7907	Cushing's syndrome
			7908	Acromegaly
			7909	Diabetes insipidus
			7911	Addison's disease (adrenocortical insufficiency)
			7916	Hyperpituitarism
			7917	Hyperaldosteronism

Table B.1—Continued

System	Our Name for the System	Direction	VASRD	VASRD Description
The endocrine system, continued	Endocrine, continued	Tightening, continued	7918	Pheochromocytoma
			7919	C-cell hyperplasia, thyroid
2010				
The musculoskeletal system: shoulder and arm	Elbow	Tightening	5201	Arm, limitation of motion
			5206[g]	Forearm, limitation of flexion
			5207[g]	Forearm, limitation of extension
			5208[g]	Forearm, flexion limited
			5213[g]	Supination and pronation, impairment
The skin	Skin and cellular	Loosening	7806	Dermatitis or eczema
The musculoskeletal system: the foot	Orthotics	Loosening	5276	Flatfoot, acquired
			5277	Weak foot, bilateral
			5278	Claw foot (pes cavus), acquired
			5279	Metatarsalgia, anterior (Morton's disease)
			5280	Hallux valgus
			5281	Hallux rigidus
			5282	Hammer toe
			5283	Tarsal or metatarsal bones
			5284	Foot injuries, other

SOURCES: Codes and descriptions are from VA, 2018b. Definitions of groups XIII and XIV are from VA, 2018a.

[a] 38 C.F.R. Part 4 lists this under miscellaneous muscle injuries.

[b] The C.F.R. lists this under the genitourinary system.

[c] The C.F.R. lists this under pelvic girdle and thigh muscle injuries.

[d] Group XIII muscles are the posterior thigh and hamstring: biceps femoris, semimembranosus, and semitendonosus.

[e] Group XIV muscles are anterior thigh muscles: sartorius, rectus femoris, and quadriceps.

[f] The C.F.R. lists this under hemic and lymphatic systems.

[g] The C.F.R. lists this under the elbow and forearm musculoskeletal system.

Descriptive Statistics and Regression Coefficients

Table C.1 contains descriptive statistics for the FY 2002–2006 accession cohorts used in our analysis. Tables C.2 through C.5 detail regression coefficients from regressions of selected medical discharge accession changes, by service.

Table C.1
Descriptive Statistics for the 2004 and 2005 Analytic Cohorts (Fiscal Year 2002–2006 Accession Cohorts)

Variable	Air Force	Army	Marine Corps	Navy
Female	0.221	0.164	0.065	0.167
Age	23.287	24.165	22.187	23.083
BMI	23.633	24.796	24.496	24.341
Ever deployed	0.402	0.576	0.544	0.434
Deployed three years ago	0.118	0.194	0.194	0.120
Cumulative months deployed as of three years ago	0.903	2.533	1.447	1.017
Number of deployments as of three years ago	0.478	0.647	0.625	0.441
Married	0.385	0.390	0.346	0.342
West MEPS at accession	0.472	0.457	0.456	0.469
Race and ethnicity				
White, non-Hispanic	0.718	0.652	0.683	0.541
Black, non-Hispanic	0.141	0.162	0.082	0.175
Other, non-Hispanic	0.064	0.014	0.051	0.068
Hispanic	0.078	0.172	0.184	0.216
Education				
Less than high school	0.001	0.007	0.002	0.014
High school	0.880	0.867	0.954	0.908

Table C.1—Continued

Variable	Air Force	Army	Marine Corps	Navy
More than high school	0.119	0.126	0.044	0.078
AFQT				
0–30 (categories IVA–V)	0.024	0.049	0.011	0.002
31–49 (category IIIB)	0.182	0.282	0.300	0.296
50–64 (category IIIA)	0.283	0.262	0.268	0.264
65–92 (category II)	0.442	0.343	0.372	0.373
93–100 (category I)	0.070	0.063	0.049	0.066
Pay grade				
E-1–E-3	0.460	0.403	0.512	0.490
E-4	0.335	0.384	0.325	0.292
E-5–E-6	0.205	0.211	0.162	0.218
E-7–E-9	0.000	0.002	0.000	0.000
Occupation				
Air Force				
Aircraft armament systems, munition, nuclear weapons	0.05			
Avionics, aerospace	0.18			
Basic airman	0.17			
Communications, computer	0.08			
Electrical, engineering, emergency management	0.06			
Flight crew, aircraft loadmaster	0.03			
Intelligence	0.05			
Medical	0.02			
Navigation, air traffic control	0.04			
Security forces	0.12			
Supply	0.02			
Transportation	0.04			
Army				
Armor		0.05		
Aviation		0.04		

Table C.1—Continued

Variable	Air Force	Army	Marine Corps	Navy
Communication		0.06		
Corps of Engineers, construction		0.04		
Field artillery and gunnery		0.06		
Food service, supply, and logistics		0.12		
Infantry		0.18		
Intelligence		0.05		
Medical		0.08		
Medics and equipment maintenance		0.09		
Marine Corps				
Artillery			0.03	
Aviation			0.15	
Infantry			0.25	
Tank or amphibious assault vehicle			0.02	
Transport or GCM			0.24	
Air Force				
Aviation				0.28
Electronics technician, engineman, hull technician, or machinist				0.27
Health				0.08
Logistics specialist, construction, or utilitiesman				0.11
Seaman				0.12
Other	0.16	0.22	0.32	0.14
Missing			0.00	0.00

NOTE: All variables are measured as 0/1 indicators, except age, BMI, cumulative months deployed, and number of deployments, which are continuous. Variables measured as indicators represent the percentage of observations for which the condition is true (e.g., percentage of observations who are female). Numbers reported for continuous variables represent averages (e.g., average age across observations was 23.287 years old). GCM = communications, construction, and transport.

Table C.2
Regression Coefficients from Regressions of Selected Medical Discharge Accession Changes, Active-Component Enlisted Air Force

Variable	Knee (2005)	Hearing (2005)	Asthma (2004)	Abdominal (2005)	Skin (2005)	Orthotics (2010)
Female	0.000043	0.000212**	0.000028	0	0.000400***	0.00213***
	(0.000150)	(0.000101)	(0.000081)	(0.000118)	(0.000126)	(0.000356)
Age	0.000013	0.000007	-0.000002	-0.000002	0.000046	0.000184***
	(0.000009)	(0.000005)	(0.000003)	(0.000005)	(0.000037)	(0.000045)
BMI	0.000058***	0.000029**	0.000027**	-0.000017	-0.000007	0.000038
	(0.000014)	(0.000011)	(0.000013)	(0.000018)	(0.000011)	(0.000025)
Ever deployed	0.000058	0.000265*	-0.000041	-0.000043	0.000074	-0.000171
	(0.000064)	(0.000138)	(0.000252)	(0.000162)	(0.000089)	(0.000137)
Deployed three years ago	0.000211**	-0.000154	0.000341	0.000144	0.000059	0.000103
	(0.000094)	(0.000184)	(0.000432)	(0.000151)	(0.000125)	(0.000302)
Cumulative months deployed as of three years ago	0.000016	0.000123**	0.000105	-0.000015	0.000035*	0.000063
	(0.000016)	(0.000047)	(0.000072)	(0.000015)	(0.000020)	(0.000057)
Total number of deployments as of three years ago	-0.000060**	-0.000320***	-0.000497***	-0.000043	-0.000138**	-0.000134*
	(0.000024)	(0.000090)	(0.000114)	(0.000072)	(0.000059)	(0.000078)
Married	-0.000009	0.000127	0.000169	0.000187*	0.000096	0.000268
	(0.000096)	(0.000081)	(0.000101)	(0.000106)	(0.000124)	(0.000206)
West MEPS at accession	-0.000601	-0.001140*	-0.000021	0.000631	0.000759	-0.000157
	(0.000657)	(0.000589)	(0.000040)	(0.00109)	(0.000730)	(0.000115)

Table C.2—Continued

Variable	Knee (2005)	Hearing (2005)	Asthma (2004)	Abdominal (2005)	Skin (2005)	Orthotics (2010)
Race (white, non-Hispanic omitted)						
Hispanic	0.000029	0.000009	0.000117	-0.000071	0.000201	0.000904
	(0.000177)	(0.000212)	(0.000193)	(0.000225)	(0.000334)	(0.000756)
Black, non-Hispanic	-0.000057	-0.000164	-0.000003	-0.000262	-0.000088	0.000308
	(0.000116)	(0.000105)	(0.000138)	(0.000177)	(0.000139)	(0.000229)
Other race, non-Hispanic	-0.000166	-0.000165	-0.000046	-0.000015	-0.000131	-0.000311
	(0.000153)	(0.000121)	(0.000121)	(0.000157)	(0.000152)	(0.000303)
Education (high school omitted)						
Less than high school	0.00181	0.005390	-0.000123	-0.000214	-0.000246	-0.000882
	(0.00171)	(0.005780)	(0.000075)	(0.000164)	(0.000287)	(0.000569)
More than high school	-0.000020	-0.000043	-0.000035	-0.000094	-0.000068	-0.000395
	(0.000224)	(0.000159)	(0.000130)	(0.000192)	(0.000216)	(0.000338)
AFQT (93–100 [category I] omitted)						
0–30 (categories IVA–V)	-0.000980***	0.000072	0.000058	-0.000194	-0.000458*	-0.001220**
	(0.000324)	(0.000142)	(0.000139)	(0.000202)	(0.000249)	(0.000473)
31–49 (category IIIB)	-0.000473*	0.000154	0.000235	-0.000204	0.000301	0.000754***
	(0.000278)	(0.000152)	(0.000149)	(0.000249)	(0.000256)	(0.000259)
50–64 (category IIIA)	-0.000271	0.000106	0.000284*	0.000016	0.000149	0.000438**
	(0.000268)	(0.000143)	(0.000159)	(0.000254)	(0.000122)	(0.000202)

100 The Relationship Between Disability Evaluation and Accession Medical Standards

Table C.2—Continued

Variable	Knee (2005)	Hearing (2005)	Asthma (2004)	Abdominal (2005)	Skin (2005)	Orthotics (2010)
65–92 (category II)	-0.000317	0.000152	0.000114	-0.000007	0.000061	0.000522***
	(0.000233)	(0.000140)	(0.000137)	(0.000239)	(0.000132)	(0.000171)
Pay grade (E-4 omitted)						
E-1–E-3	0.000756***	0.000454***	-0.000189	-0.000223	-0.000209	-0.000654
	(0.000251)	(0.000164)	(0.000209)	(0.000275)	(0.000157)	(0.001180)
E-5–E-6	-0.000080	-0.000401	-0.000379	0	0.000032	-0.001460
	(0.000189)	(0.000310)	(0.000286)	(0.000378)	(0.000299)	(0.00127)
E-7–E-9	-0.000471	-0.000420	-0.000712***	0.009330	0.009380	-0.001210
	(0.000317)	(0.000367)	(0.000264)	(0.009730)	(0.009760)	(0.001650)
Occupation (other omitted)						
Aircraft armament systems, munition, nuclear weapons	0.000456	0.000710*	-0.000066	0.000283	-0.000242	-0.000704*
	(0.000428)	(0.000416)	(0.000265)	(0.000731)	(0.000335)	(0.000402)
Avionics, aerospace	0.000570**	0.000781**	0.000351	-0.000002	-0.000022	0.000110
	(0.000252)	(0.000315)	(0.000279)	(0.000476)	(0.000290)	(0.000459)
Basic airman	-0.000499***	-0.000502*	-0.000500**	-0.00173***	-0.000444*	-0.000464
	(0.000185)	(0.000263)	(0.000198)	(0.000367)	(0.000243)	(0.000402)
Communications, computer	0.000289	-0.000064	-0.000100	-0.000221	-0.000278	-0.000656
	(0.000279)	(0.000174)	(0.000188)	(0.000536)	(0.000269)	(0.000458)
Electrical, engineering, emergency management	0.000956*	-0.000091	0.000557	-0.00105***	0.000193	-0.000113
	(0.000496)	(0.000162)	(0.000494)	(0.000361)	(0.000447)	(0.000569)

Table C.2—Continued

Variable	Knee (2005)	Hearing (2005)	Asthma (2004)	Abdominal (2005)	Skin (2005)	Orthotics (2010)
Flight crew, aircraft loadmaster	-0.000028	0.000711	-0.000043	-0.000795	0.000575	-0.000812**
	(0.000159)	(0.000457)	(0.000153)	(0.000502)	(0.000605)	(0.000337)
Intelligence	0.000896	0.000208	0.000539	-0.000258	-0.000195	-0.000584
	(0.000589)	(0.000256)	(0.000488)	(0.000638)	(0.000398)	(0.000595)
Medical	-0.000124	-0.000235	0.000105	-0.000830	0.000211	-0.00101
	(0.000098)	(0.000146)	(0.000414)	(0.000553)	(0.000908)	(0.000825)
Navigation, air traffic control	-0.000039	-0.000102	0.000125	-0.000302	-0.000515**	0.000243
	(0.000095)	(0.000147)	(0.000351)	(0.000688)	(0.000200)	(0.000736)
Security forces	0.000392	0.000443	-0.000051	-0.000479	-0.000336	-0.000211
	(0.000251)	(0.000298)	(0.000228)	(0.000470)	(0.000255)	(0.000541)
Supply	0.000942	0.001170	0.000385	-0.000617	0.000033	-0.00141***
	(0.000968)	(0.000977)	(0.000680)	(0.000482)	(0.000663)	(0.000362)
Transportation	0.000581	0.000932**	0.000594	-0.000848**	-0.000278	-0.000296
	(0.000422)	(0.000454)	(0.000481)	(0.000339)	(0.000309)	(0.000764)
Observations	951,549	951,549	935,904	929,747	951,549	763,839
R-squared	0.005	0.008	0.025	0.006	0.004	0.006

NOTE: Robust standard errors are in parentheses. The unit of analysis is the soldier-year. All regressions also include FY fixed effects, accession FY fixed effects, months-of-service cubic polynomial, months-of-service cubic polynomial interacted with the accession medical standard regime, accession MEPS fixed effect, and occupation × pay grade interaction terms. We also included BMI^2 in the regression, but the coefficients were too small to report. When significant, the effect was negative. *** $p < 0.01$; ** $p < 0.05$; * $p < 0.1$.

Table C.3
Regression Coefficients from Regressions of Selected Medical Discharge Accession Changes, Active-Component Enlisted Army

Variable	Knee (2005)	Hearing (2005)	Asthma (2004)	Abdominal (2005)	Skin (2005)	Orthotics (2010)
Female	-0.000212***	-0.000043	0.000386	-0.000023	-0.000054	0.000848***
	(0.000075)	(0.000088)	(0.000298)	(0.000055)	(0.000117)	(0.000207)
Age	0.000003	0.000007	0.000002	0.000001	0.000004	0.000097***
	(0.000003)	(0.000006)	(0.000004)	(0.000001)	(0.000003)	(0.000022)
BMI	0.000024**	0.000033***	0.000134***	0.000004	0.000043**	0.000009
	(0.000011)	(0.000011)	(0.000028)	(0.000006)	(0.000017)	(0.000015)
Ever deployed	0.000475***	0.001000***	-0.000892***	-0.000111	0.00184***	-0.000107
	(0.000156)	(0.000162)	(0.000330)	(0.000107)	(0.000230)	(0.000158)
Deployed three years ago	0.000581***	0.001200***	0.000731***	0.000060	0.00137***	0.000271
	(0.000200)	(0.000272)	(0.000247)	(0.000094)	(0.000337)	(0.000268)
Cumulative months deployed as of three years ago	-0.000011	0.000057***	0.000089	0.000007	-0.000015	0.000038
	(0.000015)	(0.000018)	(0.000019)	(0.000008)	(0.000023)	(0.000031)
Total number of deployments as of three years ago	-0.000297***	-0.000843***	-0.000655***	-0.000117**	-0.00104***	-0.000400***
	(0.000087)	(0.000119)	(0.000134)	(0.000048)	(0.000154)	(0.000071)
Married	0.000141	0.000157**	0.00105***	0.000090**	0.000293**	0.000124
	(0.000090)	(0.000065)	(0.000220)	(0.000041)	(0.000131)	(0.000094)
West MEPS at accession	-0.000355	0.000278	-0.00105	-0.000029*	-0.000283	0.001220
	(0.000260)	(0.000620)	(0.00115)	(0.000015)	(0.000688)	(0.00170)

Table C.3—Continued

Variable	Knee (2005)	Hearing (2005)	Asthma (2004)	Abdominal (2005)	Skin (2005)	Orthotics (2010)
Race (white, non-Hispanic omitted)						
Hispanic	-0.000115	-0.000021	-0.000218	0.000089	-0.000305*	-0.000076
	(0.000170)	(0.000104)	(0.000292)	(0.000081)	(0.000160)	(0.000186)
Black, non-Hispanic	-0.000248***	-0.000390***	0.00139***	0.000029	-0.000034	0.000109
	(0.000090)	(0.000077)	(0.000311)	(0.000062)	(0.000162)	(0.000161)
Other race, non-Hispanic	-0.000192	-0.000198	0.000164	-0.000017	-0.000145	0.000254
	(0.000139)	(0.000146)	(0.000334)	(0.000096)	(0.000194)	(0.000338)
Education (high school omitted)						
Less than high school	0.000176	-0.000429***	-0.000414	-0.000144***	0.00158	0.000394
	(0.000368)	(0.000089)	(0.000666)	(0.000042)	(0.00105)	(0.000638)
More than high school[1]	-0.000088	-0.000021	-0.000532**	-0.000172***	-0.000166	-0.000197
	(0.000101)	(0.000126)	(0.000241)	(0.000052)	(0.000111)	(0.000158)
AFQT (93–100 [category I] omitted)						
0–30 (categories IVA–V)	0.000516**	0.000233	0.00168***	0.000102	0.000224	-0.000312
	(0.000241)	(0.000241)	(0.000521)	(0.000180)	(0.000429)	(0.000282)
31–49 (category IIIB)	0.000135	0.000200	0.000384	-0.000174	-0.000080	-0.000206
	(0.000136)	(0.000138)	(0.000278)	(0.000115)	(0.000257)	(0.000233)
50–64 (category IIIA)	0.000352**	0.000169	0.000253	-0.000106	0.000232	-0.000042
	(0.000159)	(0.000129)	(0.000262)	(0.000101)	(0.000255)	(0.000196)

Table C.3—Continued

Variable	Knee (2005)	Hearing (2005)	Asthma (2004)	Abdominal (2005)	Skin (2005)	Orthotics (2010)
65–92 (category II)	0.000312***	0.000137	0.000463	-0.000084	0.000070	0.000002
	(0.000106)	(0.000118)	(0.000277)	(0.000104)	(0.000235)	(0.000219)
Pay grade (E-4 omitted)						
E-1–E-3	-0.000504***	-0.000435***	0.000003	-0.000183**	-0.00118***	0.000335*
	(0.000142)	(0.000095)	(0.000308)	(0.000070)	(0.000236)	(0.000179)
E-5–E-6	-0.000584***	-0.000433***	-0.00157***	-0.000074	-0.00116***	-0.000812***
	(0.000170)	(0.000148)	(0.000187)	(0.000072)	(0.000269)	(0.000207)
E-7–E-9	-0.00112***	-0.000333	-0.00235***	-0.000275***	-0.00174***	-0.001570***
	(0.000120)	(0.000579)	(0.000261)	(0.000064)	(0.000344)	(0.000447)
Occupation (other omitted)						
Armor	0.000688*	0.000217	-0.000409	0.000062	0.00125**	0.000437
	(0.000397)	(0.000272)	(0.000579)	(0.000202)	(0.000518)	(0.000357)
Aviation	-0.000419*	-0.000326	-0.000315	-0.000130	-0.00116***	-0.000232
	(0.000214)	(0.000260)	(0.000591)	(0.000117)	(0.000312)	(0.000147)
Communication	-0.000414	0.000193	-0.000740	-0.000360	-0.000975	-0.000299
	(0.000513)	(0.000117)	(0.000920)	(0.000322)	(0.000927)	(0.000328)
Corps of Engineers, construction	-0.000281	0.000466	-0.000451	-0.000093	0.00129*	0.000052
	(0.000255)	(0.000429)	(0.000506)	(0.000109)	(0.000760)	(0.000292)
Field artillery or gunnery	0.000328	0.000093	0.00128*	0.000089	0.000859	0.000502
	(0.000394)	(0.000343)	(0.000704)	(0.000255)	(0.000564)	(0.000354)

Table C.3—Continued

Variable	Knee (2005)	Hearing (2005)	Asthma (2004)	Abdominal (2005)	Skin (2005)	Orthotics (2010)
Food service, supply, and logistics	-0.000095	-0.000024	-0.000329	-0.000030	-0.000162	0.000082
	(0.000114)	(0.000117)	(0.000324)	(0.000068)	(0.000147)	(0.000088)
Infantry	0.000945***	0.000526***	0.000090	0.000071	0.00174***	0.000170**
	(0.000147)	(0.000141)	(0.000277)	(0.000075)	(0.000197)	(0.000080)
Intelligence	-0.000533***	-0.000298	-0.000483	-0.000122	-0.00112***	-0.000291**
	(0.000158)	(0.000216)	(0.000556)	(0.000102)	(0.000259)	(0.000109)
Mechanics and equipment maintenance	0.000305**	0.000146	-0.000812***	-0.000038	0.000312	0.000004
	(0.000134)	(0.000140)	(0.000278)	(0.000089)	(0.000243)	(0.000108)
Medical	-0.000539***	-0.000008	0.000627	0.000158	-0.00121***	-0.000262*
	(0.000122)	(0.000300)	(0.000749)	(0.000268)	(0.000320)	(0.000140)
Observations	2,204,536	2,204,536	2,188,494	2,152,099	2,204,536	1,944,186
R-squared	0.005	0.004	0.009	0.001	0.008	0.006

NOTE: Robust standard errors are in parentheses. The unit of analysis is the soldier-year. All regressions also include FY fixed effects, accession FY fixed effects, months-of-service cubic polynomial, months-of-service cubic polynomial interacted with the accession medical standard regime, accession MEPS fixed effect, and occupation × pay grade interaction terms. We also included BMI^2 in the regression, but the coefficients were too small to report. When significant, the effect was negative. *** $p < 0.01$; ** $p < 0.05$; * $p < 0.1$.

Table C.4
Regression Coefficients from Regressions of Selected Medical Discharge Accession Changes, Active-Component Enlisted Marine Corps

Variable	Knee (2005)	Hearing (2005)	Asthma (2004)	Abdominal (2005)	Skin (2005)	Orthotics (2010)
Female	0.000139	0.000223	0.00113	0.000148	0.000807	0.000704
	(0.000937)	(0.000784)	(0.000975)	(0.000783)	(0.000827)	(0.000577)
Age	-0.000300***	-0.000236***	-0.000283***	-0.000270***	-0.000266***	0.000148**
	(0.000079)	(0.000066)	(0.000074)	(0.000071)	(0.000073)	(0.000073)
BMI	0.000042	0.000030	0.000034	0.000021	0.000025	0.000002
	(0.000033)	(0.000024)	(0.000023)	(0.000021)	(0.000022)	(0.000006)
Ever deployed	-0.004820***	-0.004430***	-0.005080***	-0.004850***	-0.004070***	-0.000379
	(0.000597)	(0.000484)	(0.000540)	(0.000510)	(0.000568)	(0.000448)
Deployed in three years ago	-0.00272***	-0.002260***	-0.002630***	-0.002430***	-0.002330***	0.000333
	(0.000377)	(0.000236)	(0.000354)	(0.000295)	(0.000312)	(0.000848)
Cumulative months deployed as of three years ago	0.000290***	0.000173***	0.000199***	0.000208***	0.000210***	0.000429***
	(0.00005)	(0.000026)	(0.000035)	(0.000034)	(0.000037)	(0.000125)
Total number of deployments as of three years ago	-0.00128***	-0.000949***	-0.001170***	-0.001040***	-0.001220***	-0.002570***
	(0.000184)	(0.000142)	(0.000152)	(0.000149)	(0.000191)	(0.000357)
Married	-0.000388	-0.000392	-0.000140	-0.000482	-0.000571*	0.000847**
	(0.000293)	(0.000293)	(0.000404)	(0.000298)	(0.000314)	(0.000357)
West MEPS at accession	-0.000967	-0.001160	-0.002080	-0.001570	0.001590	-0.004620
	(0.002430)	(0.002450)	(0.002880)	(0.002460)	(0.004260)	(0.003250)

Table C.4—Continued

Variable	Knee (2005)	Hearing (2005)	Asthma (2004)	Abdominal (2005)	Skin (2005)	Orthotics (2010)
Race (white, Non-Hispanic omitted)						
Hispanic	-0.001560***	-0.001370***	-0.001610***	-0.001380***	-0.001180**	-0.000894**
	(0.000488)	(0.000431)	(0.000494)	(0.000402)	(0.000459)	(0.000388)
Black, non-Hispanic	-0.002180***	-0.001710***	-0.001220*	-0.001880***	-0.001360**	-0.001190***
	(0.000575)	(0.000536)	(0.000657)	(0.000616)	(0.000570)	(0.000411)
Other race, non-Hispanic	-0.000321	-0.000150	-0.000620	-0.000420	-0.000308	0.000338
	(0.000566)	(0.000479)	(0.000470)	(0.000505)	(0.000503)	(0.000544)
Education (high school omitted)						
Less than high school	-0.004300***	-0.003700***	-0.000695	-0.003880***	-0.003920***	0.001360
	(0.000449)	(0.000401)	(0.003880)	(0.000426)	(0.000429)	(0.005480)
More than high school	-0.000646	-0.000157	0.000034	0.000034	-0.000351	-0.000326
	(0.000685)	(0.000663)	(0.000723)	(0.000716)	(0.000657)	(0.000649)
AFQT (93–100 [category I] omitted)						
0–30 (categories IVA–V)	0.000836	0.000704	0.000922	0.000831	0.000134	0.001910
	(0.001700)	(0.001640)	(0.001890)	(0.002030)	(0.001660)	(0.001290)
31–49 (category IIIB)	0.000023	0.000049	-0.000213	-0.000263	-0.000359	-0.000211
	(0.000765)	(0.000703)	(0.000803)	(0.000779)	(0.000780)	(0.000671)
50–64 (category IIIA)	-0.000004	0.000137	0.000078	-0.000047	-0.000113	0.000093
	(0.000755)	(0.000690)	(0.000760)	(0.000745)	(0.000684)	(0.000566)

Table C.4—Continued

Variable	Knee (2005)	Hearing (2005)	Asthma (2004)	Abdominal (2005)	Skin (2005)	Orthotics (2010)
65–92 (category II)	0.000166	0.000133	0.000024	-0.000078	-0.000355	0.000173
	(0.000738)	(0.000712)	(0.000744)	(0.000793)	(0.000735)	(0.000626)
Pay grade (E-4 omitted)						
E-1–E-3	0.004620**	0.003420*	0.005740**	0.003610*	0.003720*	0.006850***
	(0.001970)	(0.002030)	(0.002300)	(0.001950)	(0.001980)	(0.001640)
E-5–E-6	0.001040	-0.001610	0.000129	0.000575	-0.000308	0.004760*
	(0.001850)	(0.001150)	(0.001140)	(0.001700)	(0.001230)	(0.002640)
E-7–E-9	-0.003600**	-0.002320*	-0.002630*	-0.002340*	-0.002730	0.000431
	(0.001480)	(0.001300)	(0.001320)	(0.001340)	(0.001700)	(0.003360)
Occupation (other omitted)						
Artillery	0.002540**	0.002260*	0.001740	0.001890*	0.001930*	0.001850
	(0.001110)	(0.001180)	(0.001040)	(0.001110)	(0.001080)	(0.001130)
Aviation	-0.000617	-0.000831**	-0.000677*	-0.000950**	-0.000967***	-0.000953**
	(0.000441)	(0.000345)	(0.000401)	(0.000410)	(0.000346)	(0.000450)
Infantry	0.001270**	0.000926**	0.001500***	0.000886**	0.001890***	0.001090**
	(0.000521)	(0.000424)	(0.000529)	(0.000440)	(0.000503)	(0.000509)
Tank or amphibious assault vehicle	0.003270*	0.001960	0.002590	0.003050*	0.004020*	0.003850**
	(0.001770)	(0.001470)	(0.001570)	(0.001640)	(0.002070)	(0.001700)
Transport GCM	0.001120**	0.000731	0.001040*	0.000917*	0.001010**	0.000879
	(0.000466)	(0.000445)	(0.000519)	(0.000524)	(0.000493)	(0.000547)

Table C.4—Continued

Variable	Knee (2005)	Hearing (2005)	Asthma (2004)	Abdominal (2005)	Skin (2005)	Orthotics (2010)
Missing	–0.004160	–0.002910	–0.003860	–0.003340	–0.003370	–0.003440
	(0.003110)	(0.003030)	(0.003380)	(0.003500)	(0.002930)	(0.003510)
Observations	986,369	986,369	989,650	976,824	986,369	1,152,225
R-squared	0.14	0.12	0.15	0.13	0.12	0.008

NOTE: Robust standard errors are in parentheses. The unit of analysis is the soldier-year. All regressions also include FY fixed effects, accession FY fixed effects, months-of-service cubic polynomial, months-of-service cubic polynomial interacted with the accession medical standard regime, accession MEPS fixed effect, and occupation × pay grade interaction terms. We also included BMI^2 in the regression, but the coefficients were too small to report and none was significant. *** $p < 0.01$; ** $p < 0.05$; * $p < 0.1$.

Table C.5
Regression Coefficients from Regressions of Selected Medical Discharge Accession Changes, Active-Component Enlisted Navy

Variable	Knee (2005)	Hearing (2005)	Asthma (2004)	Abdominal (2005)	Skin (2005)	Orthotics (2010)
Female	0.002130***	0.00173***	0.00191***	0.00202***	0.00186***	0.000760**
	(0.000405)	(0.000398)	(0.000424)	(0.000469)	(0.000392)	(0.000328)
Age	0.000113**	0.000132**	0.000111**	0.000062	0.000112**	0.000022
	(0.000048)	(0.000051)	(0.000051)	(0.000052)	(0.000047)	(0.000023)
BMI	0.000082***	0.000056**	0.000040	0.000034	0.000058**	0.000037**
	(0.000030)	(0.000028)	(0.000029)	(0.000030)	(0.000027)	(0.000016)
Ever deployed	-0.002780***	-0.002560***	-0.002760***	-0.002140***	-0.002620***	-0.001670***
	(0.000345)	(0.000357)	(0.000371)	(0.000368)	(0.000369)	(0.000287)
Deployed three years ago	-0.000315	-0.000200	-0.000024	0.000019	-0.000107	-0.000588
	(0.000220)	(0.000242)	(0.000291)	(0.000341)	(0.000257)	(0.000508)
Cumulative months deployed as of three years ago	0.000023	0.000007	0.000003	0.000061**	-0.000008	0.000345***
	(0.000028)	(0.000024)	(0.000027)	(0.000028)	(0.000021)	(0.000085)
Total number of deployments as of three years ago	-0.000485***	-0.000505***	-0.000551***	-0.000960***	-0.000464***	-0.000689***
	(0.000099)	(0.000090)	(0.000115)	(0.000154)	(0.000109)	(0.000146)
Married	-0.000240	-0.000110	0.000018	-0.000230	-0.000164	0.000335
	(0.000215)	(0.000218)	(0.000244)	(0.000259)	(0.000209)	(0.000210)
West MEPS at accession	-0.000305	-0.000355	-0.000304	0.000014	0.001520	0.001000
	(0.003850)	(0.003840)	(0.003870)	(0.004180)	(0.004400)	(0.002190)

Table C.5—Continued

Variable	Knee (2005)	Hearing (2005)	Asthma (2004)	Abdominal (2005)	Skin (2005)	Orthotics (2010)
Race (white, non-Hispanic omitted)						
Hispanic	-0.001120***	-0.001150***	-0.001250***	-0.001410***	-0.001130***	-0.000067
	(0.000326)	(0.000314)	(0.000320)	(0.000317)	(0.000307)	(0.000239)
Black, non-Hispanic	-0.001410***	-0.001380***	-0.001170***	-0.001460***	-0.001450***	-0.001310***
	(0.000356)	(0.000312)	(0.000340)	(0.000391)	(0.000301)	(0.000270)
Other race, non-Hispanic	-0.000045	0.000085	0.000133	-0.000116	-0.000012	-0.000534**
	(0.000367)	(0.000357)	(0.000375)	(0.000354)	(0.000353)	(0.000238)
Education (high school omitted)						
Less than high school	0.002200	0.002310	0.002780	0.002240	0.002310	-0.001290
	(0.001640)	(0.001630)	(0.001840)	(0.001680)	(0.001650)	(0.00120)
More than high school	0.000135	-0.000283	-0.000517	0.000248	-0.000342	-0.000010
	(0.000584)	(0.000532)	(0.000497)	(0.000627)	(0.000495)	(0.000349)
AFQT (93–100 [category I] omitted)						
0–30 (categories IVA–V)	-0.001490**	0.001770	-0.001670***	-0.001760**	-0.001640***	-0.001950***
	(0.000589)	(0.004050)	(0.000577)	(0.000662)	(0.000525)	(0.000492)
31–49 (category IIIB)	-0.000781	-0.001420**	-0.000991	-0.001080	-0.000957*	-0.000682
	(0.000625)	(0.000641)	(0.000595)	(0.000641)	(0.000569)	(0.000481)
50–64 (category IIIA)	-0.000541	-0.001160*	-0.000803	-0.000547	-0.000695	-0.000123
	(0.000590)	(0.000630)	(0.000586)	(0.000647)	(0.000553)	(0.000426)

Table C.5—Continued

Variable	Knee (2005)	Hearing (2005)	Asthma (2004)	Abdominal (2005)	Skin (2005)	Orthotics (2010)
65–92 (category II)	-0.000162	-0.000894	-0.000316	-0.000557	-0.000438	-0.000399
	(0.000518)	(0.000568)	(0.000507)	(0.000571)	(0.000482)	(0.000362)
Pay grade (E-4 omitted)						
E-1–E-3	0.004070***	0.004280***	0.004360***	0.004200***	0.004180***	0.003480***
	(0.000636)	(0.000638)	(0.000658)	(0.000712)	(0.000635)	(0.000572)
E-5–E-6	-0.002030***	-0.001800***	-0.001770***	-0.001920***	-0.001660***	-0.002020***
	(0.000421)	(0.000413)	(0.000421)	(0.000499)	(0.000422)	(0.000441)
E-7–E-9	-0.003020**	-0.005980*	-0.002300*	-0.002440*	-0.002470**	0.001710*
	(0.001180)	(0.003480)	(0.001260)	(0.001390)	(0.001190)	(0.000888)
Occupation (ship system omitted)						
Aviation	-0.002060***	-0.002160***	-0.002050***	-0.002430***	-0.002280***	-0.002360***
	(0.000567)	(0.000492)	(0.000529)	(0.000631)	(0.000532)	(0.000637)
Health	-0.002070**	-0.002210***	-0.001780**	-0.002480***	-0.002270***	-0.002400***
	(0.000782)	(0.000717)	(0.000755)	(0.000809)	(0.000727)	(0.000814)
Logistics specialist, construction, or utilitiesman	-0.001460***	-0.001570***	-0.001270**	-0.001330**	-0.001510***	-0.001250**
	(0.000533)	(0.000521)	(0.000572)	(0.000604)	(0.000535)	(0.000605)
Seaman	0.001990**	0.002240***	0.002430***	0.001640	0.002180***	0.001720
	(0.000838)	(0.000800)	(0.000892)	(0.001240)	(0.000762)	(0.001320)
Other	-0.001470*	-0.000997	-0.001040	-0.002260***	-0.001280*	-0.002200***
	(0.000765)	(0.000755)	(0.000765)	(0.000735)	(0.000755)	(0.000775)

Table C.5—Continued

Variable	Knee (2005)	Hearing (2005)	Asthma (2004)	Abdominal (2005)	Skin (2005)	Orthotics (2010)
Missing	−0.001500*	−0.001970***	−0.001950***	−0.002090**	−0.002140***	−0.002000**
	(0.000865)	(0.000650)	(0.000691)	(0.000949)	(0.000667)	(0.000951)
Observations	1,191,197	1,191,197	1,181,199	1,172,352	1,191,197	1,267,171
R-squared	0.08	0.08	0.08	0.10	0.08	0.06

NOTE: Robust standard errors are in parentheses. The unit of analysis is the soldier-year. All regressions also include FY fixed effects, accession FY fixed effects, months-of-service cubic polynomial, months-of-service cubic polynomial interacted with the accession medical standard regime, accession MEPS fixed effect, and occupation × pay grade interaction terms. We also included BMI^2 in the regression, but the coefficients were too small to report. When significant, the effect was negative. *** $p < 0.01$; ** $p < 0.05$; * $p < 0.1$.

Additional Accession Cohort Characteristics

In Chapter Three, we reported the percentage of medical retirements who have disability ratings for a set of common VASRD codes (Table 3.1). We also showed the percentage of each group of accessions who were medically retired in the first four and eight YOS (Figures 3.4 and 3.5). To provide a complete picture of all medical discharges, Tables D.1 and D.2 show companion data (for Table 3.1) for all medical discharges (any disability rating) and only medical separations (overall DoD disability ratings of less than 30 percent), respectively. Then, in Figures D.1 through D.4, we show the percentage of each accession group who were medically discharged (regardless of disability rating) and the percentage who were medically separated by the end of the fourth and eighth YOS.

Table D.1
Percentage of Medical Discharges (Any Disability Rating) for the Most-Frequent Conditions in the First Eight Years of Service, by Service, Accession Cohorts for Fiscal Years 2002 Through 2007

Condition	Army (46,862 Disability Separations)	Marine Corps (11,467 Disability Separations)	Navy (7,480 Disability Separations)	Air Force (7,879 Disability Separations)
Any MS	71.2	54.3	47.6	49.5
Lower MS	13.4	15.8	13.0	13.3
Knee	2.2	3.1	2.2	3.2
Any psychiatric	25.3	25.1	23.9	29.2
PTSD	16.5	16.9	6.9	10.5
Asthma	3.3	2.0	1.6	9.8
Colitis	0.8	1.4	3.7	3.5
Migraine	3.2	2.5	2.5	6.1
Epilepsy	0.9	2.0	3.5	2.8
TBI	4.5	5.0	1.6	2.0
None of the above	10.1	16.2	18.9	14.1

NOTE: Percentages can sum to more than 100 because each condition can have multiple VASRD codes.

Table D.2
Percentage of Medical Separations (Overall Department of Defense Disability Rating of Less Than 30 Percent) with the Most-Frequent Conditions in the First Eight Years of Service, by Service, Accession Cohorts for Fiscal Years 2002 Through 2007

Condition	Army (25,393 Disability Separations)	Marine Corps (5,622 Disability Separations)	Navy (3,497 Disability Separations)	Air Force (2,688 Disability Separations)
Any MS	83.7	74.2	69.2	62.8
Lower MS	14.4	20.6	18.7	17.3
Knee	2.0	3.4	2.5	3.9
Any psychiatric	5.6	7.0	10.3	11.6
PTSD	2.6	2.6	1.2	1.0
Asthma	1.1	1.7	1.3	6.7
Colitis	0.4	0.7	1.1	3.1
Migraine	1.0	0.7	1.5	2.8
Epilepsy	0.5	0.9	1.6	3.1
TBI	0.8	1.9	0.6	0.3
None of the above	9.7	14.5	15.1	15.6

NOTE: Percentages can sum to more than 100 because each condition can have multiple VASRD codes.

Figure D.1
Percentage of the Accession Cohort with Medical Discharge (Any Disability Rating) in the First Four Years of Service, by Service and Accession Fiscal Year

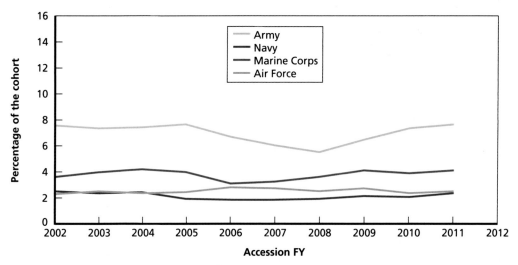

SOURCE: USMEPCOM and disability data (VTA, PDCAPS, JDETS, MilPDS).
NOTE: The reported outcome is the percentage of each accession cohort who were medically discharged (with any overall DoD disability rating) anytime during the first four years of service. Those who were accessioned in FY 2011 were the most-recent service members we could follow for four years.

Figure D.2
Percentage of the Accession Cohort with Medical Discharge (Any Disability Rating) in the First Eight Years of Service, by Service and Accession Fiscal Year

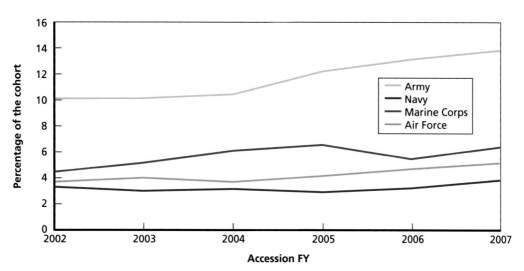

SOURCES: USMEPCOM and disability data (VTA, PDCAPS, JDETS, MilPDS).
NOTE: The reported outcome is the percentage of each accession cohort who were medically separated (with an overall DoD disability rating of less than 30 percent) anytime during the first eight years of service. Those who were accessioned in FY 2007 were the most-recent service members we could follow for eight years.

Figure D.3
Percentage of the Accession Cohort with Medical Separation (Overall DoD Disability Rating of Less Than 30 Percent) in the First Four Years of Service, by Service and Accession Fiscal Year

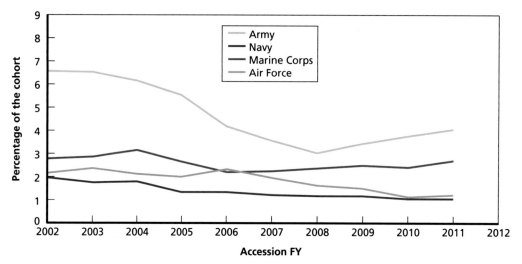

SOURCES: USMEPCOM and disability data (VTA, PDCAPS, JDETS, MilPDS).
NOTE: The reported outcome is the percentage of each accession cohort who were medically separated (with an overall DoD disability rating of less than 30 percent) anytime during the first four years of service. Those who were accessioned in FY 2011 were the most-recent service members we could follow for four years.

Figure D.4
Percentage of the Accession Cohort with Medical Separation (Overall DoD Disability Rating of Less Than 30 Percent) in the First Eight Years of Service, by Service and Accession Fiscal Year

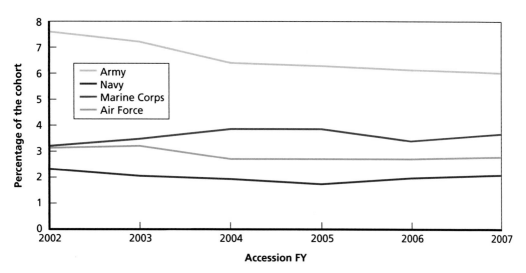

SOURCES: USMEPCOM and disability data (VTA, PDCAPS, JDETS, MilPDS).
NOTE: The reported outcome is the percentage of each accession cohort who were medically separated (with an overall DoD disability rating of less than 30 percent) anytime during the first eight years of service. Those who were accessioned in FY 2007 were the most-recent service members we could follow for eight years.

We now turn to PULHES scores. Figures D.5 through D.10 show the percentage of each accession cohort with PULHES scores greater than 1 (where a score of 1 indicates a high level of medical fitness and 4 indicates a medical condition that is severe enough to cause drastically limited military duty), by service and by PULHES category. Then, Figures D.11 through D.14 show the percentage of each group of accessions with medical failure codes from the physical exam for psychiatric, abdominal, lower extremity, and skin conditions. These are four areas that experienced changes in accession medical standards during the period we studied.

Figure D.5
Percentage of the Accession Cohort with Physical (P) PULHES Scores Greater Than 1, 12-Month Rolling Average, by Service and Fiscal Year

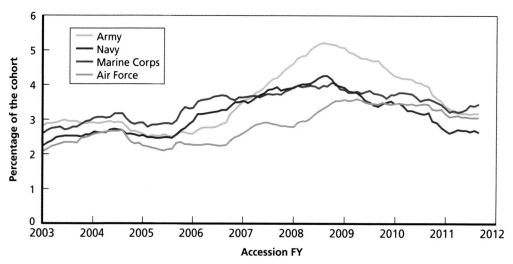

SOURCE: USMEPCOM data.

Figure D.6
Percentage of the Accession Cohort with Upper Extremity (U) PULHES Scores Greater Than 1, 12-Month Rolling Average, by Service and Fiscal Year

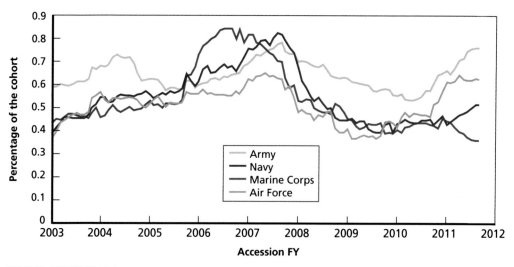

SOURCE: USMEPCOM data.

Figure D.7
Percentage of the Accession Cohort with Lower Extremity (L) PULHES Scores Greater Than 1, 12-Month Rolling Average, by Service and Fiscal Year

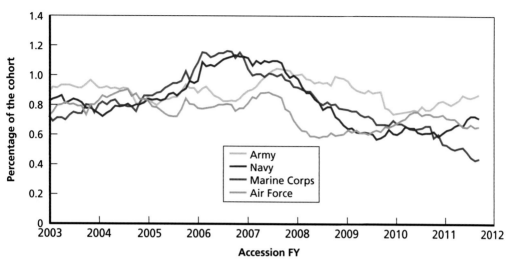

SOURCE: USMEPCOM data.

Figure D.8
Percentage of the Accession Cohort with Hearing (H) PULHES Scores Greater Than 1, 12-Month Rolling Average, by Service and Fiscal Year

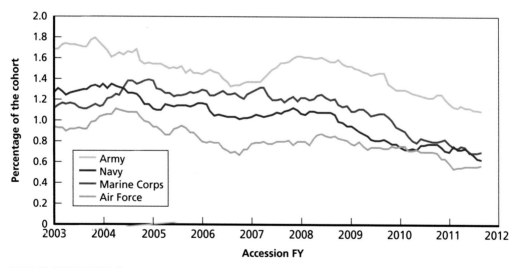

SOURCE: USMEPCOM data.

Figure D.9
Percentage of the Accession Cohort with Eyes (E) PULHES Scores Greater Than 1, 12-Month Rolling Average, by Service and Fiscal Year

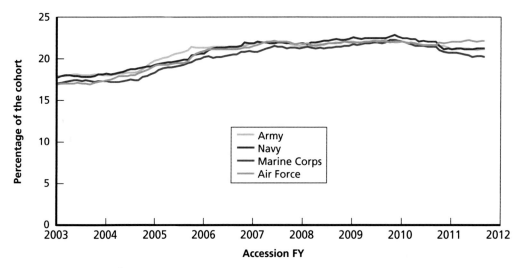

SOURCE: USMEPCOM data.

Figure D.10
Percentage of the Accession Cohort with Psychiatric (S) PULHES Scores Greater Than 1, 12-Month Rolling Average, by Service and Fiscal Year

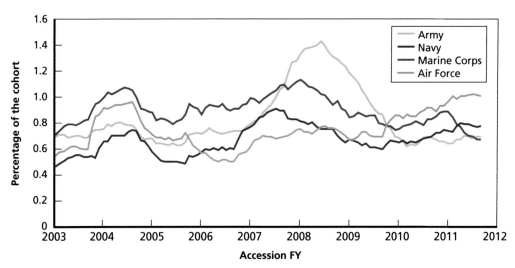

SOURCE: USMEPCOM data.

Figure D.11
Percentage of the Accession Cohort with Psychiatric Failure Codes, 12-Month Rolling Average, by Service and Fiscal Year

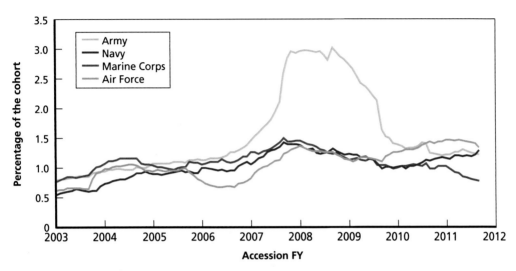

SOURCE: USMEPCOM data.

Figure D.12
Percentage of the Accession Cohort with Abdominal Failure Codes, 12-Month Rolling Average, by Service and Fiscal Year

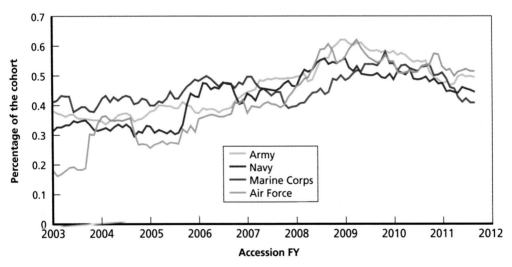

SOURCE: USMEPCOM data.

Figure D.13
Percentage of the Accession Cohort with Lower Extremity Failure Codes, 12-Month Rolling Average, by Service and Fiscal Year

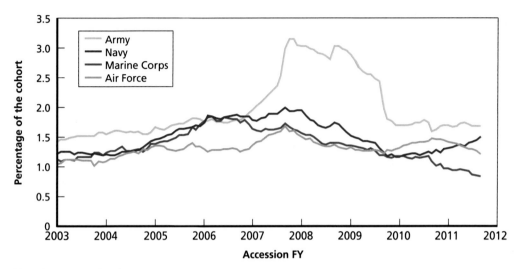

SOURCE: USMEPCOM data.

Figure D.14
Percentage of the Accession Cohort with Skin-Related Failure Codes, 12-Month Rolling Average, by Service and Fiscal Year

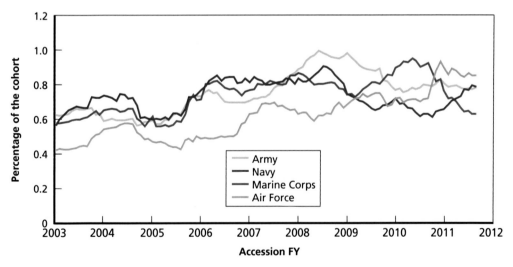

SOURCE: USMEPCOM data.

Sensitivity Analyses

Sensitivity Analyses of the Relationship Between Accession Medical Standards and Medical Discharges

In Chapter Three, we presented the estimated effects that accession medical standard changes have on accumulated medical discharges related to those medical changes, five years later, for those discharging with combined DoD disability ratings of at least 30 percent. This appendix contains corresponding eight-year estimates for medical discharges with at least 30-percent disability ratings (Figure E.1). In addition, we show five- and eight-year estimates for medical discharges regardless of rating (Figures E.2 and E.3), as well as medical separations for those who receive disability ratings of less than 30 percent (Figures E.4 and E.5).

Figure E.1
The Effect That Accession Medical Standard Changes Have on the Eight-Year Medical Discharge Rate with at Least 30-Percent Ratings

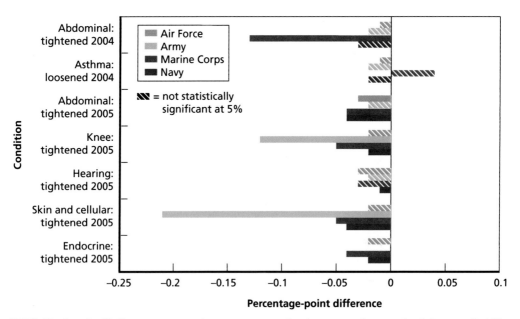

NOTE: The bars in this figure represent the percentage-point decrease or increase in eight-year disability retirements (disability rating of 30 percent or higher) for the postaccession change cohort, relative to the prechange cohort. The eight-year disability retirement rate is the percentage of the cohort who were medically retired by the end of the eighth YOS. Solid bars represent statistically significant effects at 1 percent or 5 percent. Diagonally shaded bars represent effects that were not statistically significant at 5 percent.

Figure E.2
The Effect That Accession Medical Standard Changes Have on the Five-Year Medical Discharge Rate, Any Disability Rating

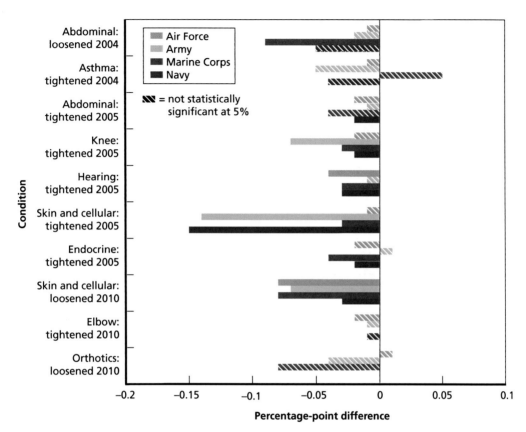

NOTE: The bars in this figure represent the percentage-point decrease or increase in five-year medical discharges (any disability rating) for the postaccession change cohort, relative to the prechange cohort. The five-year medical discharge rate is the percentage of the cohort who were medically discharged by the end of the fifth YOS. Solid bars represent statistically significant effects at 1 percent or 5 percent. Diagonally shaded bars represent effects that were not statistically significant at 5 percent.

Figure E.3
The Effect That Accession Medical Standard Changes Have on the Eight-Year Medical Discharge Rate, Any Disability Rating

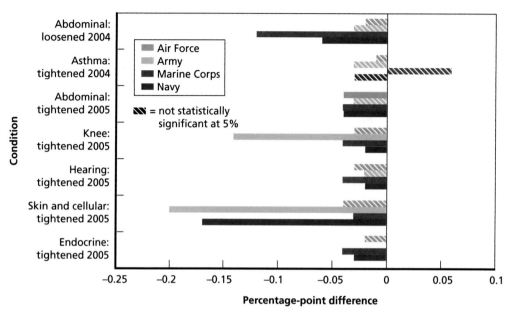

NOTE: The bars in this figure represent the percentage-point decrease or increase in eight-year medical discharges (any disability rating) for the postaccession change cohort, relative to the prechange cohort. The eight-year medical discharge rate is the percentage of the cohort who were medically discharged by the end of the eighth YOS. Solid bars represent statistically significant effects at 1 percent or 5 percent. Diagonally shaded bars represent effects that were not statistically significant at 5 percent.

Figure E.4
The Effect That Accession Medical Standard Changes Have on the Five-Year Disability Separation Rate, Disability Rating of Less Than 30 Percent

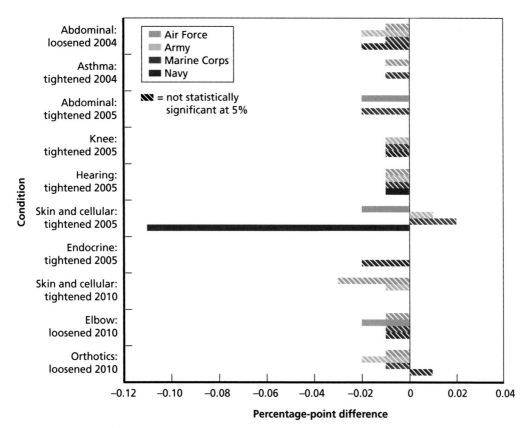

NOTE: The bars in this figure represent the percentage-point decrease or increase in five-year disability separations (disability rating of less than 30 percent) for the postaccession change cohort, relative to the prechange cohort. The five-year disability separation rate is the percentage of the cohort who were medically separated by the end of the fifth YOS. Solid bars represent statistically significant effects at 1 percent or 5 percent. Diagonally shaded bars represent effects that were not statistically significant at 5 percent.

Figure E.5
The Effect That Accession Medical Standard Changes Have on the Eight-Year Disability Separation Rate, Disability Rating of Less Than 30 Percent

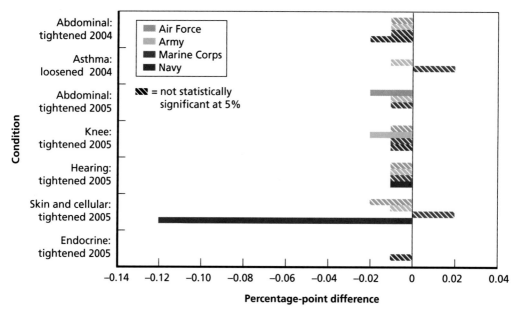

NOTE: The bars in this figure represent the percentage-point decrease or increase in eight-year disability separations (disability rating of less than 30 percent) for the postaccession change cohort, relative to the prechange cohort. The eight-year disability separation rate is the percentage of the cohort who were medically separated by the end of the eighth YOS. Solid bars represent statistically significant effects at 1 percent or 5 percent. Diagonally shaded bars represent effects that were not statistically significant at 5 percent.

Cost Estimate Sensitivity Analyses

In Chapter Four, we presented baseline cost estimates for statistically significant effects among the ten policy changes under study and across all four services, where baseline is defined as the following characteristics:

- The age of enlistees in the first year of service is 19.
- Medical retirement or separation cannot occur after someone has 19 completed YOS.
- The three-year estimate of a policy's effect on disability retirements is evenly distributed across the first three years (shape 2).

Using our cost model, we varied these three assumptions, and Table E.1 presents the range of cost estimates for each policy change, first repeating the baseline estimate from Table 4.2 in Chapter Four.

Table E.1
Minimum and Maximum per-Recruit Cost Estimates Associated with Medical Standard Changes in the First Five Years of Service, in Dollars

Condition	Army		Marine Corps		Navy		Air Force	
	Baseline	Range	Baseline	Range	Baseline	Range	Baseline	Range
2004								
Abdominal			−481	−461 to −559	−149	−143 to −172		
Asthma							−151	−141 to −160
2005								
Knee	−433	−393 to −458	−212	−197 to −225	−103	−97 to −110		
Abdominal			−190	−175 to −201	−166	−158 to −188		
Hearing								
Skin and cellular	−894	−831 to −945	−323	−301 to −341	−194	−181 to −207		
Endocrine			−219	−211 to −254				
2010								
Elbow	−302	−290 to −346	−385	−367 to −433	−167	−160 to −194	−325	−313 to −387
Skin and cellular								
Orthotics								

NOTE: The range of cost estimates reported in this table represents the findings from a variety of sensitivity analyses. First, our baseline model assumed that all active-component enlistees were 19 years of age at the time of accession and that medical retirement or separation could not occur after someone has 19 completed YOS. We relaxed both of those assumptions (allowing someone to enlist at any age between 19 and 22 and allowing medical discharge at year 2C). In addition, our Chapter Three model produced three-, four-, and five-year rates of medical discharge. Our cost model requires estimates at each year of service, including years 1 and 2. Our baseline model smooths the three-year estimates over years 1 and 2, and our sensitivity analyses used twc additional approaches: (1) smoothing the five-year estimate evenly across all five years and (2) taking the three sets of estimates as given, which means there is no change in disability outcomes in years 1 and 2, and all of the effects happen in years 3, 4, and 5. We also based the model on current health care consumption patterns, which dip around age 40. In one assumption, we fixed health care consumption between ages 40 and 65.

References

Accession Medical Standards Analysis and Research Activity, homepage, last modified April 1, 2015. As of September 30, 2018:
http://www.amsara.amedd.army.mil/

Air Force Research Oversight and Compliance, Air Force Medical Service, *Medical Service: Medical Evaluation Boards (MEB) and Continued Military Service*, Washington, D.C., Air Force Instruction 44-157, December 12, 2000. As of October 7, 2018:
https://webapp1.dlib.indiana.edu/virtual_disk_library/index.cgi/821003/FID177/pubs/af/44/afi44-157/afi44-157.pdf

AMSARA—*See* Accession Medical Standards Analysis and Research Activity.

"Army Integrated Disability Evaluation System (IDES)," webpage, undated. As of January 30, 2019:
https://www.army.mil/e2/rv5_downloads/features/readyandresilient/ARMY_IDES.pdf

Asch, Beth J., Paul Heaton, James Hosek, Paco Martorell, Curtis Simon, and John T. Warner, *Cash Incentives and Military Enlistment, Attrition, and Reenlistment*, Santa Monica, Calif.: RAND Corporation, MG-950-OSD, 2010. As of September 29, 2018:
https://www.rand.org/pubs/monographs/MG950.html

Asch, Beth J., Michael G. Mattock, and James Hosek, *Reforming Military Retirement: Analysis in Support of the Military Compensation and Retirement Modernization Commission*, Santa Monica, Calif.: RAND Corporation, RR-1022-MCRMC, 2015. As of September 29, 2018:
https://www.rand.org/pubs/research_reports/RR1022.html

Assistant Secretary of Defense for Force Management Policy, *Physical Disability Evaluation*, Washington, D.C., Department of Defense Instruction 1332.38, November 14, 1996. As of September 30, 2018:
https://biotech.law.lsu.edu/blaw/dodd/corres/pdf/i133238_111496/i133238p.pdf

———, *DoD Physical Fitness and Body Fat Programs Procedures*, Washington, D.C., Department of Defense Instruction 1308.3, November 5, 2002. As of October 7, 2018:
https://biotech.law.lsu.edu/blaw/dodd/corres/pdf/i13083_110502/i13083p.pdf

Camarca, Margaret M., and Margot R. Krauss, "Active Tuberculosis Among U.S. Army Personnel, 1980 to 1996," *Military Medicine*, Vol. 166, No. 5, 2001, pp. 452–456.

Clark, Kathryn L., M. René Howell, Yuanhzung Li, Timothy Powers, Kelly T. McKee Jr., Thomas C. Quinn, Joel C. Gaydos, and Charlotte A. Gaydos, "Hospitalization Rates in Female US Army Recruits Associated with a Screening Program for *Chlamydia Trachomatis*," *Sexually Transmitted Diseases*, Vol. 29, No. 1, January 2002, pp. 1–5.

Clark, Kathryn L., Yuanzhang Li, Margot R. Krauss, and Patrick W. Kelley, "The Asthma Accession Standard: A Survival Analysis of Military Recruits, 1995 to 1997," *Military Medicine*, Vol. 165, No. 11, November 2000, pp. 852–854.

Code of Federal Regulations, Title 38, Pensions, Bonuses, and Veterans' Relief; Chapter I, Department of Veterans Affairs; Part 4, Schedule for Rating Disabilities. As of January 20, 2019: https://www.govinfo.gov/app/details/CFR-2016-title38-vol1/CFR-2016-title38-vol1-part4

Commandant of the Marine Corps, *Military Personnel Procurement Manual*, Vol. 2: *Enlisted Procurement (Short Title: MPPM ENLPROC)*, Washington, D.C., Marine Corps Order P1100.72C, February 10, 2004. As of October 7, 2018: https://www.marines.mil/Portals/59/Publications/MCO%20P1100.72C%20W%20ERRATUM.pdf

———, *Marine Corps Body Composition and Military Appearance Program*, Washington, D.C., Marine Corps Order 6110.3, August 8, 2008. As of October 7, 2018: https://www.marines.mil/Portals/59/Publications/MCO%206110.3%20W%20CH%201.pdf

———, *Separation and Retirement Manual (Short Title: MARCORSEPMAN)*, Washington, D.C., Marine Corps Order 1900.16, change 1, August 7, 2015. As of October 7, 2018: https://www.marines.mil/News/Publications/MCPEL/Electronic-Library-Display/Article/900480/mco-190016-wch-1/

———, "Conduct of Recruiting Operations," Washington, D.C., Marine Corps Order 1130.76D, March 7, 2017. As of October 7, 2018: https://www.marines.mil/News/Publications/MCPEL/Electronic-Library-Display/Article/1110701/mco-113076d/

Commanding General, Marine Corps Recruiting Command, *Marine Corps Recruiting Command Enlistment Processing Manual (Short Title: MCRC EPM)*, Washington, D.C., Marine Corps Recruiting Command Order 1100.1, November 9, 2011. As of October 7, 2018: https://www.hqmc.marines.mil/Portals/61/Docs/FOIA/MCRCO1100.1EPM.pdf

Congressional Budget Office, *Approaches to Reducing Federal Spending on Military Health Care*, Washington, D.C., January 16, 2014. As of October 1, 2018: https://www.cbo.gov/publication/44993

Cox, Karin A., Kathryn L. Clark, Yuanzhang Li, Timothy Powers, and Margot R. Krauss, "Prior Knee Injury and Risk of Future Hospitalization and Discharge from Military Service," *American Journal of Preventive Medicine*, Vol. 18, No. 3, Suppl. 1, April 2000, pp. 112–117.

Defense Finance and Accounting Service, military pay chart for 2015, January 1, 2015. As of October 1, 2018: https://www.dfas.mil/dam/jcr:b6ef41d4-f071-45f9-b863-70b202be05a6/2015MilitaryPayChart_2.pdf

Defense Health Board, *DHB Implications of Trends in Obesity and Overweight for the DoD: Fit to Fight Fit, for Life*, Falls Church, Va., November 22, 2013. As of September 30, 2018: http://www.dtic.mil/docs/citations/AD1027323

Deputy Chief of Staff of the Air Force for Manpower, Personnel and Services, Accession and Training Management Division, *Personnel: Enlisted Accessions*, Washington, D.C., Air Force Instruction 36-2002, July 11, 2017. As of October 7, 2018: http://static.e-publishing.af.mil/production/1/af_a1/publication/afi36-2002/afi36-2002.pdf

Director of Medical Operations and Research, Surgeon General, Headquarters, U.S. Air Force, *Aerospace Medicine: Medical Examinations and Standards*, Washington, D.C., Air Force Instruction 48-123, November 5, 2013, with changes through January 28, 2018. As of October 2, 2018:
http://static.e-publishing.af.mil/production/1/af_sg/publication/afi48-123/afi48-123.pdf

Directorate of Personnel Services, Air Force's Personnel Center, *Personnel: Physical Evaluation for Retention, Retirement, and Separation*, Joint Base San Antonio–Randolph, Texas, Air Force Instruction 36-3212, February 2, 2006, incorporating through change 2, November 27, 2009. As of October 7, 2018:
http://static.e-publishing.af.mil/production/1/af_a1/publication/afi36-3212/afi36-3212.pdf

———, *Personnel: Fitness Program*, Washington, D.C., Air Force Instruction 36-2905, October 21, 2013, incorporating change 1, August 27, 2015. As of October 7, 2018:
https://www.afpc.af.mil/Portals/70/documents/Home/AF%20Fitness%20Program/AFI%2036-2905_FITNESS%20PROGRAM.pdf

Elmasry, Hoda, Michael R. Boivin, Xiaoshu Feng, Elizabeth R. Packnett, and David N. Cowan, "Preenlistment and Early Service Risk Factors for Traumatic Brain Injury in the Army and Marine Corps: FY 2002–2010," *Journal of Head Trauma Rehabilitation*, Vol. 32, No. 1, January–February 2017, pp. E1–E7.

Gubata, Marlene E., Elizabeth R. Packnett, Xiaoshu Feng, David N. Cowan, and David W. Niebuhr, "Pre-Enlistment Hearing Loss and Hearing Loss Disability Among US Soldiers and Marines," *Noise and Health*, Vol. 15, No. 66, September–October 2013, pp. 289–295.

Gubata, Marlene E., Elizabeth R. Packnett, and David N. Cowan, "Temporal Trends in Disability Evaluation and Retirement in the Army, Navy, and Marine Corps: 2005–2011," *Disability and Health Journal*, Vol. 7, No. 1, January 2014, pp. 70–77.

Gubata, Marlene E., Amanda L. Piccirillo, Elizabeth R. Packnett, David W. Niebuhr, Michael R. Boivin, and David N. Cowan, "Risk Factors for Back-Related Disability in the US Army and Marine Corps," *Spine*, Vol. 39, No. 9, April 20, 2014, pp. 745–753.

Headquarters, Department of the Army, *Medical Services: Standards of Medical Fitness*, Washington, D.C., Army Regulation 40-501, March 28, 2002a.

———, *Medical Services: Standards of Medical Fitness*, Washington, D.C., Army Regulation 40-501, September 30, 2002b.

———, *Medical Services: Standards of Medical Fitness*, Washington, D.C., Army Regulation 40-501, August 29, 2003.

———, *Medical Services: Standards of Medical Fitness*, Washington, D.C., Army Regulation 40-501, February 15, 2004a.

———, *Medical Services: Standards of Medical Fitness*, Washington, D.C., Army Regulation 40-501, February 19, 2004b.

———, *Medical Services: Standards of Medical Fitness*, Washington, D.C., Army Regulation 40-501, April 12, 2004c.

———, *Medical Services: Standards of Medical Fitness*, Washington, D.C., Army Regulation 40-501, February 1, 2005.

———, *Medical Services: Standards of Medical Fitness*, Washington, D.C., Army Regulation 40-501, February 16, 2006a.

———, *Medical Services: Standards of Medical Fitness*, Washington, D.C., Army Regulation 40-501, June 27, 2006b.

————, *Medical Services: Standards of Medical Fitness*, Washington, D.C., Army Regulation 40-501, January 18, 2007a.

————, *Medical Services: Standards of Medical Fitness*, Washington, D.C., Army Regulation 40-501, May 29, 2007b.

————, *Medical Services: Standards of Medical Fitness*, Washington, D.C., Army Regulation 40-501, December 14, 2007c.

————, *Medical Services: Standards of Medical Fitness*, Washington, D.C., Army Regulation 40-501, December 14, 2007, rapid action revision, September 10, 2008.

————, *Medical Services: Standards of Medical Fitness*, Washington, D.C., Army Regulation 40-501, December 14, 2007, rapid action revision, August 23, 2010.

————, *Medical Services: Standards of Medical Fitness*, Washington, D.C., Army Regulation 40-501, December 14, 2007, rapid action revision, August 4, 2011.

————, *Personnel—General: The Army Body Composition Program*, Washington, D.C., Army Regulation 600-9, June 28, 2013. As of October 7, 2018: http://www.armyg1.army.mil/hr/bodyComposition/docs/AR600_9_28-June-2013.pdf

————, *Personnel Separations: Disability Evaluation for Retention, Retirement, or Separation*, Washington, D.C., Army Regulation 635-40, January 19, 2017a.

————, *Medical Services: Standards of Medical Fitness*, Washington, D.C., Army Regulation 40-501, June 14, 2017b. As of September 29, 2018: https://armypubs.army.mil/ProductMaps/PubForm/Details.aspx?PUB_ID=1002549

Hosek, James, Beth J. Asch, and Michael G. Mattock, *Toward Efficient Military Retirement Accrual Charges*, Santa Monica, Calif.: RAND Corporation, RR-1373-A, 2017. As of September 29, 2018: https://www.rand.org/pubs/research_reports/RR1373.html

Hosek, James, Beth J. Asch, Michael G. Mattock, Italo A. Gutierrez, Patricia K. Tong, and Felix Knutson, *An Assessment of the Military Survivor Benefit Plan*, Santa Monica, Calif.: RAND Corporation, RR-2236-OSD, 2018. As of September 29, 2018: https://www.rand.org/pubs/research_reports/RR2236.html

Hosek, James, and Trey Miller, *Effects of Bonuses on Active Component Reenlistment Versus Prior Service Enlistment in the Selected Reserve*, Santa Monica, Calif.: RAND Corporation, MG-1057-OSD, 2011. As of September 29, 2018: https://www.rand.org/pubs/monographs/MG1057.html

Krauss, Margot R., Robert K. Russell, Timothy E. Powers, and Luanzhang Li, "Accession Standards for Attention-Deficit/Hyperactivity Disorder: A Survival Analysis of Military Recruits, 1995–2000," *Military Medicine*, Vol. 171, No. 2, February 2006, pp. 99–102.

Mastrobuoni, Giovanni, "Labor Supply Effects of the Recent Social Security Benefit Cuts: Empirical Estimates Using Cohort Discontinuities," *Journal of Public Economics*, Vol. 93, No. 11–12, December 2009, pp. 1224–1233.

NAVMED—*See* Navy Bureau of Medicine and Surgery.

Navy Bureau of Medicine and Surgery, U.S. Navy, *Change 126, Manual of the Medical Department, U.S. Navy*, Washington, D.C., Navy Bureau of Medicine and Surgery P-117, June 11, 2001.

————, *Change 116, Manual of the Medical Department, U.S. Navy*, Washington, D.C., Navy Bureau of Medicine and Surgery P-117, August 12, 2005.

————, *Manual of the Medical Department (MANMED)*, Washington, D.C., Navy Bureau of Medicine and Surgery P-117, updated June 1, 2018a. As of October 2, 2018:
https://www.med.navy.mil/directives/Pages/NAVMEDP-MANMED.aspx#

————, *Change 166, Manual of the Medical Department, U.S. Navy*, Washington, D.C., Navy Bureau of Medicine and Surgery P-117, December 20, 2018b.

Navy Wounded Warrior–Safe Harbor, "Disability Evaluation System," undated. As of October 1, 2018:
https://www.navywoundedwarrior.com/recovery/disability-evaluation-system

Niebuhr, David W., Rebekah L. Krampf, Jonathan A. Mayo, Caitlin D. Blandford, Lynn I. Levin, and David N. Cowan, "Risk Factors for Disability Retirement Among Healthy Adults Joining the U.S. Army," *Military Medicine*, Vol. 176, No. 2, February 1, 2011, pp. 170–175.

Niebuhr, David W., Yuanzhang Li, Timothy E. Powers, Margot R. Krauss, David Chandler, and Thomas Helfer, "Attrition of U.S. Military Enlistees with Waivers for Hearing Deficiency, 1995–2004," *Military Medicine*, Vol. 172, No. 1, January 1, 2007, pp. 63–69.

OACT—*See* Office of the Actuary.

Office of the Actuary, U.S. Department of Defense, *Statistical Report on the Military Retirement System: Fiscal Year 2013*, July 2014. As of October 5, 2018:
https://actuary.defense.gov/Portals/15/Documents/
MRS_StatRpt_2013_July.pdf?ver=2014-07-16-110305-087

————, *Statistical Report on the Military Retirement System: Fiscal Year 2014*, June 2015. As of October 5, 2018:
https://actuary.defense.gov/Portals/15/Documents/
MRS_StatRpt_2014.pdf?ver=2015-06-24-072935-040

————, *Statistical Report on the Military Retirement System: Fiscal Year 2015*, July 2016a. As of October 1, 2018:
https://actuary.defense.gov/Portals/15/Documents/
MRS_StatRpt_2015%20Final%20v2.pdf?ver=2016-07-26-162207-987

————, *Valuation of the Medicare-Eligible Retiree Health Care Fund, September 30, 2015*, December 2016b. As of October 1, 2018:
https://actuary.defense.gov/Portals/15/Documents/
MERHCF%20Val%20Rpt%202015.pdf?ver=2016-12-28-073724-523

————, *Actuarial Work for the Chief Financial Officers Act (CFO) Financial Statements (MERHCF, SMA, CRM, DHA, DoD Agency-Wide)*, file memorandum, January 2017. As of October 1, 2018:
https://actuary.defense.gov/Portals/15/Documents/Documentation%20of%209-30-16%20PRB%20
results%20for%20CFO%20financial%20statements_final.pdf?ver=2017-01-25-153133-897

Office of the Assistant Secretary of Defense for Health Affairs, *Criteria and Procedure Requirements for Physical Standards for Appointment, Enlistment, or Induction in the Armed Forces*, Department of Defense Instruction 6130.4, December 14, 2000.

————, *Criteria and Procedure Requirements for Physical Standards for Appointment, Enlistment, or Induction in the Armed Forces*, Washington, D.C., Department of Defense Instruction 6130.4, April 2, 2004a. As of September 29, 2018:
https://biotech.law.lsu.edu/blaw/dodd/corres/pdf/i61304_040204/i61304p.pdf

————, "Medical Records Retention and Coding at Military Treatment Facilities," Washington, D.C., Department of Defense Directive 6040.41, April 13, 2004b. As of October 7, 2018:
https://biotech.law.lsu.edu/blaw/dodd/corres/pdf/d604041_041304/d604041p.pdf

Office of the Chief of Aerospace Medicine Policy and Operations, U.S. Air Force, *Aerospace Medicine: Medical Examinations and Standards*, Washington, D.C., Air Force Instruction 48-123, September 24, 2009.

Office of the Chief of Naval Operations, Department of the Navy, *Physical Readiness Program*, Washington, D.C., Office of the Chief of Naval Operations Instruction 6110.1H, August 15, 2005. As of October 7, 2018:
https://www.sc.edu/nrotc/content/Documents/6110.1H.pdf

Office of the Command Surgeon, Air Force Special Operations Command, *Aerospace Medicine: Medical Examinations and Standards*, Washington, D.C., Air Force Instruction 48-123, November 14, 2000.

———, *Aerospace Medicine: Medical Examinations and Standards*, Washington, D.C., Air Force Instruction 48-123, May 22, 2001.

———, *Aerospace Medicine: Medical Examinations and Standards*, Vol. 2: *Accession, Retention, and Administration*, Washington, D.C., Air Force Instruction 48-123 vol. 2, June 5, 2006.

Office of the Under Secretary of Defense for Personnel and Readiness, *Population Representation in the Military Services, Fiscal Year 2004*, c. 2004. As of December 27, 2018:
https://prhome.defense.gov/M-RA/Inside-M-RA/MPP/Accession-Policy/Pop-Rep/2004/

———, *Population Representation in the Military Services, Fiscal Year 2005*, c. 2005a. As of December 27, 2018:
https://prhome.defense.gov/M-RA/Inside-M-RA/MPP/Accession-Policy/Pop-Rep/2005/

———, *Medical Standards for Appointment, Enlistment, or Induction in the Armed Forces*, Washington, D.C., Department of Defense Instruction 6130.4, January 18, 2005b.

———, *Population Representation in the Military Services, Fiscal Year 2010*, c. 2010a. As of December 27, 2018:
https://prhome.defense.gov/M-RA/Inside-M-RA/MPP/Accession-Policy/Pop-Rep/2010/

———, *Deployment-Limiting Medical Conditions for Service Members and DoD Civilian Employees*, Washington, D.C., Department of Defense Instruction 6490.07, February 5, 2010b. As of September 29, 2018:
http://www.esd.whs.mil/Portals/54/Documents/DD/issuances/dodi/649007p.pdf

———, *Medical Standards for Appointment, Enlistment, or Induction in the Military Services*, Washington, D.C., Department of Defense Instruction 6130.03, April 28, 2010c.

———, *Medical Standards for Appointment, Enlistment, or Induction in the Military Services*, Washington, D.C., Department of Defense Instruction 6130.03, April 28, 2010, incorporating change 1, September 13, 2011. As of September 29, 2018:
http://www.nrotc.navy.mil/pdfs/DoDI%206130.03.pdf

———, *Qualification Standards for Enlistment, Appointment, and Induction*, Washington, D.C., Department of Defense Instruction 1304.26, March 13, 2015, incorporating change 2, April 11, 2017. As of October 7, 2018:
http://www.esd.whs.mil/Portals/54/Documents/DD/issuances/dodi/130426p.pdf

———, *Enlisted Administrative Separations*, Washington, D.C., Department of Defense Instruction 1332.14, January 27, 2014, incorporating change 3, March 22, 2018a. As of October 7, 2018:
http://www.esd.whs.mil/Portals/54/Documents/DD/issuances/dodi/133214p.pdf

————, *Commissioned Officer Administrative Separations*, Washington, D.C., Department of Defense Instruction 1332.30, May 11, 2018b. As of October 7, 2018:
http://www.esd.whs.mil/Portals/54/Documents/DD/issuances/dodi/
133230p.pdf?ver=2018-05-11-101352-010

OUSD(P&R)—*See* Office of the Under Secretary of Defense for Personnel and Readiness.

Otto, William C., David W. Niebuhr, Timothy E. Powers, Margot R. Krauss, Francis L. McVeigh, and Aaron K. Tarbett, "Attrition of Military Enlistees with a Medical Waiver for Myopia, 1999–2001," *Military Medicine*, Vol. 171, No. 11, November 1, 2006, pp. 1137–1141.

Packnett, Elizabeth R., Marlene E. Gubata, David N. Cowan, and David W. Niebuhr, "Temporal Trends in the Epidemiology of Disabilities Related to Posttraumatic Stress Disorder in the U.S. Army and Marine Corps from 2005–2010," *Journal of Traumatic Stress*, Vol. 25, No. 5, October 2012, pp. 485–493.

Page, William F., Mikayla Chubb, Xiaoshu S. Feng, Lynn Y. Fan, Yuanzhang Li, Natalya S. Weber, Lynn I. Levin, and David W. Niebuhr, "National Estimates of Seroincidence and Seroprevalence for Herpes Simplex Virus Type 1 and Type 2 Among US Military Adults Aged 18 to 29 Years," *Sexually Transmitted Diseases*, Vol. 39, No. 4, April 2012, pp. 241–250.

Piccirillo, Amanda L., Elizabeth R. Packnett, Michael R. Boivin, and David N. Cowan, "Epidemiology of Psychiatric Disability Without Posttraumatic Stress Disorder Among U.S. Army and Marine Corps Personnel Evaluated for Disability Discharge," *Journal of Psychiatric Research*, Vol. 71, December 2015, pp. 56–62.

Piccirillo, Amanda L., Elizabeth R. Packnett, David N. Cowan, and Michael R. Boivin, "Epidemiology of Asthma-Related Disability in the U.S. Armed Forces: 2007–2012," *Journal of Asthma*, Vol. 53, No. 7, September 2016, pp. 668–678.

Public Law 110-181, National Defense Authorization Act for Fiscal Year 2008, January 28, 2008. As of October 1, 2018:
https://www.gpo.gov/fdsys/pkg/PLAW-110publ181/content-detail.html

Secretary of the Navy, *Department of the Navy (DON) Disability Evaluation Manual*, Washington, D.C., Secretary of the Navy Instruction 1850.4E, April 30, 2002. As of October 7, 2018:
http://www.secnav.navy.mil/mra/CORB/Documents/SECNAVINST-1850-4E.PDF

————, *Periodic Health Assessment for Individual Medical Readiness*, Washington, D.C., Secretary of the Navy Instruction 6120.3, change 1, December 1, 2009. As of October 7, 2018:
https://www.med.navy.mil/sites/nmcphc/Documents/nepmu-6/Environmental-Health/
Health-Promotions/SECNAVINST-6120-3-CH-1.pdf

Tilghman, Andrew, "The Military May Relax Recruiting Standards for Fitness and Pot Use," *Military Times Rebootcamp*, November 1, 2016. As of September 30, 2018:
https://rebootcamp.militarytimes.com/education-transition/education/2016/11/01/
the-military-may-relax-recruiting-standards-for-fitness-and-pot-use/

U.S. Air Force Surgeon General, *Operations: Duty Limiting Conditions*, Air Force Instruction 10-203, November 20, 2014. As of October 1, 2018:
https://www.afpc.af.mil/Portals/70/documents/Home/AF%20Fitness%20Program/
Air%20Force%20Instruction%2010-203.pdf?ver=2016-12-15-132612-563

————, *Aerospace Medicine: Deployment Health*, Air Force Instruction 48-122, August 18, 2014, incorporating change 1, June 12, 2017. As of October 7, 2018:
http://static.e-publishing.af.mil/production/1/af_sg/publication/afi48-122/afi48-122.pdf

U.S. Army Medical Command, *IDES Guidebook: An Overview of the Integrated Disability Evaluation System*, July 2013. As of October 1, 2018:
http://dmna.ny.gov/hro/agr/army/files/1416862502--IDES_GUIDEBOOK_and_Ref_Guide_9_July_13.pdf

U.S. Department of Veterans Affairs, "Muscle Injuries Disability Benefits Questionnaire," Washington, D.C., Form 21-0960M-10, March 2018a. As of October 7, 2018:
https://www.vba.va.gov/pubs/forms/VBA-21-0960M-10-ARE.pdf

———, "Web Automated Reference Material System: 38 CFR Book C, Schedule for Rating Disabilities," last updated November 19, 2018b. As of January 5, 2019:
https://www.benefits.va.gov/WARMS/bookc.asp

———, "Benefit Rates," last updated December 7, 2018c. As of January 17, 2019:
https://www.benefits.va.gov/compensation/rates-index.asp

U.S. Government Accountability Office, *Military Disability System: Preliminary Observations on Efforts to Improve Performance*, Washington, D.C., GAO-12-718T, May 23, 2012. As of October 1, 2018:
https://www.gao.gov/products/GAO-12-718T

U.S. Military Entrance Processing Command, "A Day at the MEPS," undated. As of September 30, 2018:
http://www.mepcom.army.mil/About-Us/USMEPCOM-Videos/A-Day-at-the-MEPS/

VA—*See* U.S. Department of Veterans Affairs.

Vanden Brook, Tom, "Army Is Accepting More Low-Quality Recruits, Giving Waivers for Marijuana to Hit Targets," *USA Today*, October 10, 2017, updated October 11, 2017. As of September 30, 2018:
https://www.usatoday.com/story/news/politics/2017/10/10/army-accepting-more-low-quality-recruits-giving-waivers-marijuana-hit-targets/750844001/

Walter Reed Army Institute of Research, U.S. Army Medical Research and Materiel Command, "Department of Epidemiology," last modified September 9, 2016. As of September 30, 2018:
http://www.wrair.army.mil/ReAndDevelop_InfectDisRe_PreventiveMedicine_DeptOfEpidemiology.aspx